THERE'S ONLY ONE TOMMY WILSON

BEST WISHES TO JIM.
Tommy

THERE'S ONLY ONE TOMMY WILSON

Douglas Miller

foreword by David Lloyd

CHARLCOMBE BOOKS

Charlcombe Books
17 George's Road, Bath BA1 6EY
Tel 01225-335813

First published 2015

ISBN 978 0 9568510 4 8

Printed and bound in Great Britain by
CPI Antony Rowe, Bumper's Farm, Chippenham, Wilts

Contents

Foreword

by David Lloyd

Tommy Wilson. Legend. A true cricket man. Tommy had everything you need to be a top class umpire, knowledge of the laws, understanding of the game, man management ..… and his own coat!

Tommy umpired our Lancashire Second Eleven games, had a spell as a first-class umpire and officiated when I was put out to grass in minor counties cricket for Cumberland. We were in good hands.

You know the best thing about Tommy? He would always have a smile on his face and would always be there to help.

I am glad this book has been written about him, his love of cricket, his village life … I am sure there will be many good tales!

I am sure Tommy will not mind me recalling a game at Old Trafford when he was standing with Tommy Drinkwater, who had a pot arm. Tommy liked a drink. He went to the loo and came back minus his pot arm. We looked high and low for it and eventually found it in the car park in the custody of groundsman, Bert Flack's Alsatian, 'Taff'!!! Happy Days!!

Preface

It was August 2012, in the early evening of the day before the Minor Counties one-day final at Wormsley. A small group of people were sitting in the courtyard of their small hotel in Ibstone waiting for a pre-booked minibus to pick them up and take them into London.

Among the company was Tommy Wilson and the reason they were assembled was because it had become known that Tommy had never been to the theatre, and this cultural deficiency in an otherwise full and active life was about to be rectified.

Unfortunately, for whatever reason, the minibus did not appear; the group could not get to London (and as far as I know, Tommy has still not been to the theatre). With few alternatives available to them, it was decided to stay at the hotel and a table for dinner was duly booked.

The point is that whatever entertainment the theatre trip may have provided paled into insignificance compared to that served up over the dinner table and indeed for a good couple of hours afterwards. Tommy had got into full flow and simply told story after story about his life in cricket. Memories of people, places, matches, incidents tumbled out in a flood of hilarious anecdotes which left the listeners doubled up with laughter.

I joined the company the next day in the more tranquil setting of one of England's most beautiful grounds, and aside from being ribbed constantly about the non-appearance of the minibus (apparently that was my fault…..) all I heard were recollections of the night before; the extraordinary breadth of Tommy's cricketing experience and the sheer fun and laughter exuded as a result of his story telling.

Why not write it all down? Surely a book would amuse and interest all cricket lovers, particularly those whose own experience spanned the vicarious parts of the recreational game rather than the dizzy heights of professional cricket? Terry Burstow was the chief protagonist; he spent the whole day alternately chuckling and bending my ear! Thus the idea was spawned and subsequently brought into being by Douglas Miller, who having been persuaded to take on the project, combined the most diligent research with his own skills to author 'There is only one Tommy Wilson' – and here it is!

It is a well-known fact that funny and charming tales that trip off the tongue in the company of good food and a few drinks seldom translate in quite the same way to the written page, but aside from the anecdotes, Tommy's story is worth telling. It is not just the humble beginnings or the onset of polio; the battle for recognition as a 'disabled' umpire and the subsequent achievements of record number of matches officiated in League and Minor Counties; the extraordinary triumph over adversity in becoming a first-class umpire – and a highly respected one at that. The continuous administration, appointing and assessing with the travelling to watch and advise others or the most recent mentoring of a new group of youngsters who look up to him like a favourite grandfather – and hang on his every word. It is the whole unique package which is the story: I hope you enjoy it!

Nick Cousins
Chief Executive
Association of Cricket Officials

Author's Introduction and Acknowledgements

The light on my telephone was winking. I listened to the latest recorded message. It was Nick Cousins, the chief executive of the ECB ACO, the body that looks after umpires throughout recreational cricket. He had a proposition in which I might be interested. I rang back and managed to catch him – that in itself is some feat with Nick! Before long he was round at my home, enthusing me with the possibility of writing a book with an ageing umpire of whom I had never heard.

It didn't take long for Nick to whet my appetite. Over the past ten years I had enjoyed the challenge of committing to paper the stories of five prominent first-class players, each one a privilege and a pleasure. Now Nick was offering me the chance of doing the same with an umpire. Though I was daft enough to have played the game till the age of 69, umpiring had now become my principal involvement with cricket. Standing in the second division of the Thames Valley League may be the limit of my aspirations, but the white blouson and Dickie Bird cap have given me a new lease of life.

But who was Tommy Wilson? Nick allayed my ignorance, telling me of this unreformed Lancastrian who had umpired minor county cricket since the days of long coats. I learnt that, despite carrying a leg with a calliper, this was a man who had made it to the first-class list. And then there were all his stories….. As soon as I met Tommy, I knew it was a challenge I wanted to take on, just hoping I could do justice to the man of whom his many umpiring friends are quick to say, 'There's only one Tommy Wilson.' I am deeply grateful to Nick for the brilliant idea of a book, for introducing me to Tommy, for scanning through the completed text and for penning a few introductory words.

My thanks go also to the many people who have helped in my attempts to capture Tommy's story. I have spoken at length with Paul Adams and Philip August. I have met Ken Shenton at Tommy's home and Nick Ward at his school, while assistance has come from many others, some known to me, some total strangers, both umpiring colleagues of Tommy and those who have waited in fear or hope of seeing his finger rise: David Armstrong, Paddy Brown, Keith Coburn, Ben Cousins, Hughie Evans, John Hampshire, Ray Illingworth, Alan Jones, Ray Julian, Chris Kelly, Roger Knight, John Pickup, Jack Simmons, Mike Smedley, Derek Underwood, Bob White and Alan Wilson. For comments on Geoff Cope's bowling troubles I have raided the on-line work of John Ward. Where statistics are quoted, Cricket Archive has been my principal source.

To David Lloyd I am grateful for a beautifully crafted Foreword, a tribute to a man he much admired. My thanks to David's wife Diana for ensuring that it was fitted into her husband's busy schedule. My friend Stephen Chalke, recovering from an arduous year completing 'Summer's Crown', his splendid history of the County Championship, has made time to prepare the book for the printers and oversee its progress, while he has also kindly drawn it to the attention of his discerning mailing list.

Above all I am grateful to Tommy and Barbara, whose hospitality I have enjoyed and with whom I have enjoyed the pleasures of The Blue Anchor. My thanks go also to their two daughters, Hayley and Marie, for contributions and for arranging a family photograph.

I acknowledge permission kindly granted by Getty Images to use action photographs of Mike Procter and Andrew Flintoff. I am indebted to Roger Mann for allowing the use of the photograph of Joe Blackledge, and I am particularly grateful to Paul Adams, who responded to an eleventh hour call for a picture of himself by sending one that included Neil Bainton. All other photographs are from Tommy's collection or were taken by myself.

Only rarely does a book truly satisfy its author. For any errors and other deficiencies in what I am offering to readers, I alone take responsibility.

Douglas Miller
February 2015

About the author

Douglas Miller has written eight other cricket books including five of a biographical nature. The subjects with whom he has sat down to capture their stories are: for Fairfield Books, Don Shepherd and Charles Palmer, and for ACS Publications, Allan Watkins, Jack Bond and M.J.K. Smith. He is a past chairman of the Association of Cricket Statisticians and Historians, but his principal involvement with the game is now as an umpire – one whose confidence, on the eve of publication of this book, is sky high after scoring 100 % against Hawkeye!

Tommy in the shop, on the day he received the call from Lord's

Chapter One

'Get down to Headingley': Roses Match baptism

'Play.'

Tom Spencer, one of England's best-regarded Test umpires, had started the Roses Match.

At square leg, his back to Headingley's Western Terrace, stood 38-year-old Tommy Wilson. There had been no chance of play on the Saturday, but by Monday the weather had relented to allow a prompt start. With his colleague's call Tommy's dream had been fulfilled. Monday 31st May 1976 was the day on which he had become a first-class umpire. Only elevation to the Test panel could surpass this moment for a man who had played no first-class cricket – in fact no cricket at all, his aspirations to take an active part in any physical sport cruelly curtailed by a leg withered by polio, the scourge of so many youngsters of his generation .

It had all been a bit chaotic. Tommy had been at work that Friday afternoon serving the customers in his corner shop in the Lancashire village of Bretherton, when the telephone rang. Brian Langley, assistant secretary at the Test and County Cricket Board, had been relieved to find him there. 'I thought it was someone having me on,' says Tommy, recalling Langley's explanation for the purpose of his call. David Evans, another of the country's leading umpires, destined soon to take charge of Test matches, had been scheduled to stand in the Roses Match but had cried off ill. 'Get your bags packed and get down to Headingley,' said Langley, 'You're the nearest reserve umpire I have, so it's your game.'

It wasn't the baptism Tommy had expected. He had been listed for a Gillette Cup match later in the season, but until Langley's call the plan for that Saturday had been for a trip to the seaside for Blackpool's Northern League match against Preston. Now he was to be plunged into English cricket's most fiercely contested county fixture. It would be the 159th time Yorkshire and Lancashire had locked horns since the championship began in 1890, with a further 46 first-class Roses encounters before that date, the earliest as far back as 1849. Even with both counties in the lower half of the table, it would be hard to envisage a higher-profile championship match, and soon Tommy would learn that the biggest game of his life was to be on television.

There was time for the Lancashire Evening Post to make the appointment a lead story on its front page. 'When I got the telephone call from Lord's I must admit that it shook me for a few minutes,' Tommy confessed, going on to assure the reporter that he wouldn't be nervous. 'I'll treat it as a normal game,' he said. Tommy busied himself with making arrangements for the time he would be away from the shop. Then, with overnight accommodation still to be fixed up, he collected his kit together, packed an overnight bag and was on his way in his Bedford van.

He had never previously met Tom Spencer, but he found his colleague, who suggested that they should get to know each other over a few drinks. 'Come on, we'll take a walk round a few pubs and have a few halves,' Spencer said, pulling on his gabardine raincoat to brave the Leeds weather. 'Keep your money in your pocket,' Tommy's new colleague counselled. 'We're not going to pay. I know a lot of people.' Out they went. 'And we'd walk into a pub and somebody'd say "Hey there Tommy – it's Tommy Spencer, what are you having?" "Oh we'll have a couple of halves of bitter." And then we'd move on to the next pub and there were another lot waiting to buy us another couple of halves. He was a crafty sod!'

It was disappointing for Tommy that no play could take place on the Saturday, but the delay gave him the chance to read the telegrams from the Northern League and other well-wishers, as his duties never went beyond inspecting a waterlogged square. This was a time when championship matches that started on a Saturday suffered a disruptive break to accommodate a John Player League game on the Sunday. It meant Lancashire had to return to Old Trafford to play Warwickshire, while Yorkshire took on Northamptonshire at Park Avenue, Bradford. For the two umpires, also taking charge of this match, there was not far to travel. So Tommy's first outing involving two first-class counties was a 40-over affair in which Yorkshire's 202 for eight, with 87 from Richard Lumb, proved an easy target for the visitors, as Peter Willey, undefeated on 102, steered Northants to an eight-wicket win with eight balls in hand.

Tom Spencer offered helpful advice as he and Tommy prepared for the start of the Roses match. He mentioned the plans for televising the game, pointing out that Tommy would need a white shirt. 'I've got a cream one,' he replied, 'a very nice cream one, and I've got a pale blue one and the one I'm stood in.' Spencer shook his head. 'They'll not do.' It was panic stations. 'I went to the Lancashire dressing room and knocked on the door. "Eeeh, bloody hell, it's Wilson" – because they all knew me. I said, "I'm in a bit of a jam. I've not got a white shirt and I need one." So Peter Lever said, "You can have this," and he threw me a crumpled old thing. It was supposed to be white, but he'd worn it half a dozen times. I said, "I can't wear that." So Jack Simmons said, "Here's a brand new shirt in a packet – never been opened. You can wear that, Tom." I said thanks and went back to put it on.' Tommy unpacked the new shirt and pulled it on. Then he fixed his tie. Years later he leans back and chuckles. 'I'm not kidding you when I say he'd got a huge neck', and Tommy demonstrates far how he was from filling Simmons' 17 ½ inch collar.

Time in the middle on the Sunday had helped ease Tommy's nerves for the big match. Now he was back at Headingley watching Chris Old open the Yorkshire bowling to Barry Wood. The England pace man, at the peak of his powers in the mid-1970s, had a damp pitch of uncertain bounce to help him, but the batsmen might have hoped for some respite at Tommy's end where Howard Cooper, an honest county medium-pacer, was to operate. 'You take that end with the cameras,' Tom Spencer had said as they made their way to the middle, television's eagle eye being confined in those days to a single position behind the bowler at only one end with a second camera installed square with the wicket. Was this invitation – it seemed more like an instruction – from the more experienced umpire a kindness to Tommy or was it a calculated ploy by Spencer to minimise the scrutiny of his own decision-making? 'I've no idea – he was a funny chap,' Tommy replies with a chuckle nearly 40 years later, but he has always wondered.

Lancashire's decision to bat in the shortened match had seemed questionable, and any hopes that they might build a score from which to dictate the game were soon in tatters. Old, in the view of The Daily Telegraph's Mike Stevenson, produced the best bowling of the day with 'fire, length and line', but it was Cooper who was soon calling the tune. Lancashire had edged their way nervously to 19 when he first struck, bowling a leaden-footed Wood. Then within the next 16 deliveries he had claimed two more wickets without conceding a run.

Tommy's finger rose for the first time when Andrew Kennedy played back to a ball that hurried through. The Simmons shirt was playing an early part in the day's entertainment from the commentary box. 'There's a new county umpire on the panel from Chorley in Lancashire' listeners were told. 'He's just given him out with his sleeve. I couldn't see his finger, but the sleeve shot up.'

For none of the reporters covering the game was there any doubt that Tommy had made a sound decision, none resorting to the dreaded phrase that the batsman had been 'adjudged lbw'. Yet years later Kennedy could joke with Tommy about the way the ball had brushed his bat. Director of Sport at Taunton School, Kennedy brought his young teams to the English Schools tournament where Tommy officiated. 'And he used to arrive each year and he'd say, "Oh no, it's not you again! Boys, gather round, this is the man that gave me out lbw when I nicked it!" I said, "You never nicked it in a million years!"'

With Frank Hayes following Kennedy to the pavilion, bowled by Cooper for a duck, a scoreboard reading 24 for three was hardly what skipper David Lloyd had hoped to see as he joined Harry Pilling to set about repairing the innings. They took the score to 120, but the damage was done. Valuable time was ebbing from the match and with Pilling's dismissal the scoring rate decelerated. Despite Farokh Engineer breathing some life into the latter stages, 88 overs had been taken up in reaching 201 for seven. Lloyd's declaration once he had banked a second batting point left Yorkshire 19 overs to bat that evening. Barrie Leadbeater managed just three singles before the close came at 23 for one. Unless Lancashire could force a follow-on, available if they could contain Yorkshire to 101 in what had become a two-day match, there would be only bonus points for which to play. Yorkshire ground their way to 143, Leadbeater taking 200 minutes for his 28, and only Bob Ratcliffe, with five for 30, was able to look back on the final day with much satisfaction.

For most of those reporting the game it had been a futile day's cricket with the quest for bonus points negating any chance of a more positive approach from the captains. For Tom Spencer, as he departed for Trent Bridge to officiate at the Test match starting that Thursday, it had been just one more match towards a championship total of 571, the highest number of all time. For Tommy Wilson it was an umpiring experience he would cherish for the rest of his life.

By the end of the week a cheque was in the post. Brian Langley hoped that Tommy had enjoyed his first taste of the county game. The payment was £43, made up of £28 for the first-class match and £15 for standing in the John Player League. Other expenses were recouped from the Yorkshire County Club, and the John Player match also earned Tommy 400 cigarettes. A non-smoker, he was still grateful for the fags. 'We sold them in the shop!' At the 1976 price of 45 pence a packet, that was another £9 in Tommy's pocket.

Tommy had been inundated with messages of good will, but one that had a special poignancy came after the match. A cousin in the Hebrides wrote that she had been having her usual mundane afternoon, 'when Bill yelled at me to come and look at the TV. There was Tommy as large as life!' Remembering that they had met up a few months earlier, she went on to recall his prophetic words as they had parted: 'You'll be seeing me one of these days on the telly!' 'Well he was quite right', she concluded, 'We've seen him!'

Chapter Two

Early days at Bretherton

A man found guilty of treason might not inspire many in naming a child. As in so much of his life, Thomas Guy Wilson, born just before midnight on 5th November 1937, defied convention, his second name acknowledging the man whose nefarious plot to blow up parliament in 1605 was only narrowly averted. Tommy was born in the Lancashire village of Bretherton, nine miles from Preston in the borough of Chorley. The eighth and youngest child of Jenny and Hugh Wilson, Tommy never knew two of his brothers who had died in infancy. The five siblings with whom he grew up comprised three sisters and two brothers, of whom just one brother now survives, a near neighbour in the village where Tommy has spent his whole life.

The outbreak of war took Tommy's father to Liverpool, where he was involved in bomb disposal work. A pattern of life in which he would return home only at weekends continued after the war, by which time he was working as a builder in the reconstruction of Liverpool, a city ravaged by German bombs. The visits home became less regular and from the age of about nine Tommy barely set eyes on his father again. The family later discovered that Hugh had been living a double life, a mid-week mistress in Liverpool bearing him a further eight children. 'It's even rumoured that he had one more child by another woman,' Tommy relates, 'making it 17 in all.' Though his father later lived in retirement in Liverpool, he often visited his brothers and sisters in Much Hoole, a village some four miles from Bretherton. Occasionally he revisited old haunts, once bragging in a local pub that he was the only man around who was drawing his old age pension and child allowance.

'I don't remember him a lot,' Tommy says without regret, recalling how his mother struggled to make ends meet. 'A marvellous woman,' he says. 'She had a hard life, bringing us up like she did and managing – patching clothes and knitting. I don't know how she did it.' The post brought occasional envelopes with cash from her errant husband, who was soon managing a successful building business in Liverpool, but nothing on which Jenny could rely. Hugh had effectively deserted his family. There was never a divorce, Tommy's mother remaining determined to deny her husband the chance to marry his Liverpool mistress. 'Fortunately my brothers and sisters were older than me and working – that's the only way we could survive,' says Tommy. 'We always ate, but I never remember having a new suit – I just had hand-me-downs from my brothers. When one of my sisters got married, my mother went to a shop somewhere in Preston to get me a second-hand suit.'

Tommy's mother

Tommy's childhood home

Jenny was fortunate that her parents had a small farm on the edge of the village. During the war there had been a regular supply of eggs and cheese. Occasionally a pig would be killed, perhaps illegally Tommy now believes, and there would be bacon, ham and pork. The family were also lucky that Jenny had been given the large house where they all lived at the time of her wedding. They were lucky, too, that her husband had no claim to it. There was no electricity, the family relying on oil lamps and candles, and Tommy remembers that the radio – the wireless as they would have called it – relied on an accumulator 'and we had to go and get the acid for it from the chemist in the next village of Croston.' If some basic comforts were lacking, there was compensation in having space outside to breed tame rabbits for the pot, an enterprise that would help sustain the family in Tommy's adult life. 'We sold them to the hotels in Blackpool. They used them as chicken!'

Early life for Tommy would always have been tough but at the age of two he was to suffer the misfortune that was destined to shape his life, poliomyelitis. Polio or infantile paralysis, as it was commonly known at the time, was an ever-present threat to youngsters of Tommy's generation, striking suddenly and indiscriminately. Tommy remembers a brief period in an iron lung to assist his breathing. When his arms were found to be unaffected, he was released, but the disease had severely damaged his left leg, the destruction of two muscles leaving him with a shortened limb and an ankle that could no longer fulfil its function. Henceforth Tommy would be reduced to walking with a calliper. He has no memory of life without one.

The traditional outdoor sports that his friends could enjoy were denied to Tommy, but he was nevertheless attracted to cricket. There was no tradition of playing the game in the family, but when the Bretherton club, founded in 1925, resumed after the war, young Tommy was one of those doing his bit to help get it back on its feet. Facilities were primitive, he recalls, with the outfield cut twice a year and the grass allowed to grow almost a foot tall. 'They used to cut it and then bale it.' The club tried a bit harder with the square, but the mower 'wasn't that brilliant and it used to leave great strands of tough grass.'

The club was fortunate to have a captain, George Wilson, no relation of Tommy, who had an important job at County Hall in Preston. Determined to make the square as presentable as possible, the captain was generous in his encouragement of the youngsters to pluck out the errant strands of grass by hand. 'Pick up every piece of grass that's stuck up and I'll give you a shilling a bunch,' he offered them. 'A lot of money then,' says Tommy. 'It was only two shillings to watch Preston North End on a Saturday!'

Soon Tommy was recruited to do the scoring for the club. Then, when he was 11 or 12, he was entrusted with mowing the outfield. The club by now had a large motor mower to tackle the job and they acquired a seat on which Tommy could ride behind the machine. He recalls the practice evenings when the players would discard their sweaters and caps and run in to bowl in the nets. They took little heed of where Tommy wanted to come with his mower. 'I threatened them – if you don't move them, I'll run over 'em! I kept threatening them, then one day – I didn't do it on purpose – I went over this pullover. There was bits of wool flying everywhere!'

Whatever his groundsmanship skills, Tommy was soon to prove his worth as a scorer. Then, before the 1952 season, the club faced a problem – their umpire died. They turned to Tommy: would the youngster, who was only 14, be prepared to take over the white coat? It was the chance that would set him on his journey towards the first-class list. That year was a successful one for Bretherton, and they won promotion to the second division of the Southport & District League. Next summer the club would no longer be providing its own umpire – officials would be appointed from a panel. Never one to shrink from a challenge, Tommy took the plunge – he applied to join the panel. Despite his age – he was fifteen and a half – the league accepted him.

This was the year, 1953, in which Tom Smith founded the Association of Cricket Umpires (the ACU, later to become ACU&S once scorers had been brought into the fold), but several seasons would pass before his collaboration with MCC secretary, Colonel Rait Kerr, bore fruit in the form of the now familiar manual and formal training programmes. In an age where umpires were largely self-taught, Tommy made it his business to study the laws and, when the first 'Tom Smith' book came out, he was an early purchaser. Not until the winter of 1963/4 was he to attend a training course, but knowing the laws has always been one of Tommy's particular strengths. Years later he would stand at Bradford with Don Oslear, one of the few umpires to reach the Test panel without first-class playing experience and an acknowledged expert on the game's legal intricacies. 'He tested me and he said, "The two most knowledgeable umpires on the first-class list, as far as the laws are concerned, are you and me!"'

In 1948, when he was eleven and a half, the chance had arisen for Tommy to have an operation on his malformed leg. He remembers that a Mr Garden, a surgeon at Preston Hospital, had been to London and been impressed by a pioneering operation to lengthen legs. 'He put it to my mother that he would like to do this operation on my leg and at the same time fuse my ankle, which I had no control over.' Tommy's left leg was by now two and a half inches shorter than his right. The surgeon sawed through the leg, inserting steel supports with knobs. 'Each day they came and turned the knobs which lengthened the leg bit by bit,' Tommy recalls. 'There was this gap of two and a half inches with no bone. Then they waited for the bone growing, so I was in plaster for 13 weeks. They were going to take some bone from my hip and transplant it in there, but they didn't need to because the bone grew. It's only thin bone, but it has only broken once, in 2000. Then they fused the ankle.'

The surgeon had wanted to fuse Tommy's knee as well, but his mother wouldn't allow it. Had the additional surgery taken place, Tommy might have found walking easier, albeit with a stiff leg, but he would have been unable to bend his knee. So the chance of driving a car, already a daunting prospect, would have been even less likely, and the stiff leg would have made it impossible for him to sit down at the cinema. His mother's was a wise decision, he is now quite certain.

The months spent in the hospital and subsequent recuperation meant that Tommy missed two years' schooling at a crucial juncture. Though baptised as a Congregationalist, he had attended Bretherton's Church of England school where he is now chairman of governors. He remembers the early years carrying his gas mask to school each day, and he looks back on a harsh regime, where there was a ruler across the back of the hand for any misdemeanour. Yet where today's educational system would ensure provision for a boy in Tommy's predicament, there was no suggestion that he might attend classes in a wheelchair. Nor was there any special tuition or homework. Yet, before his education resumed, Tommy was propelling himself around the village with his damaged leg supported on a truck with pram wheels made for him by his brothers. 'I used to go past the school and wave at them!'

When Tommy was able to return to school, he had fallen so far behind that it came as no surprise that he should fail the exam for higher education. Leaving school with scant academic qualifications, he found temporary jobs delivering milk and driving a tractor on a friend's farm. Then he applied to work on the railway as a booking clerk, but failed the exam. Taught how to mend shoes by an uncle, Tommy found a job repairing boots and clogs at a shop in Preston. It was while serving his seven-year apprenticeship with the cobblers that Tommy first met a young lady called Barbara Sumner. A few months older than Tommy, she worked as a van driver for the company.

'Are yer courting?' Had Tommy been confronted by the catch phrase of the period immortalised by Wilfred Pickles on his popular radio show

'Have a Go', he would soon have had only one answer. When Tommy was 20, he and Barbara began to go out together. Plans for a marriage that would last well over 50 years were soon being made, though it was not until 1961 that the wedding took place. By this time they had embarked on a business together. Finding a lock-up shop in Bretherton available for 12 shillings and sixpence (62p) a week, they took the plunge and rented the premises. Shoe repairing had been part of the previous business alongside selling goods that ranged from haberdashery to birthday cards. 'We paid £80 for the stock,' Tommy recalls.

Tommy was still living with his mother when he and Barbara first decided to set up on their own, while Barbara made a daily journey from Preston by bus or on her scooter. It had been a big gamble for the young couple, but their hard work was soon rewarded. They lashed out £28 to buy a small car, a Standard 8, which enabled Barbara to drive round the outlying villages picking up shoes for repair. Tommy had always imagined that he would never be able to drive, but Barbara had other ideas. Under her tuition, and with a brick under the clutch to rest his left leg, Tommy was soon proving her right. The brick was still in place when Tommy passed his driving test. In later years he has favoured an automatic gearbox, but this was not an option when he started out. He remembers the difficulties he had with double declutching and seized brakes. 'I used to wear clutches out because I used to ride my clutch, especially when we had Bedford vans.' Then there were the problems of signalling in the days before all vehicles were fitted with indicators. 'If you were turning, you had to stick your hand out of the window.'

Upgrading the car for a hatchback, a Hillman Husky, allowed Barbara to operate a parallel business with a stall at the weekly markets at Preston and Ormskirk. 'Haberdashery, jumpers, shirts, socks, underwear, overalls, aprons, all sorts' she recalls selling, and she will never forget braving the freezing cold as she loaded and unloaded all the stock.

The couple married on 10th June 1961 at the Anglican church near Barbara's home in Preston. Situated close to Preston Cricket Club, the church is no more, while the nearby school that Barbara had attended as a child is now the site of a mosque. It was a happy day for both families, though the wedding went unacknowledged by Tommy's father, who had never visited his young son during his long months in Preston Hospital and ignored him again now. Barbara was never to meet Hugh, but there had been a close call in the local pub 'Your father's in the other bar,' Tommy had been told. 'Cancel them drinks,' he had said hastily and hustled Barbara away.

Wedding day

There was a buffet after the wedding at a nearby club, after which the newly-weds set off for their honeymoon. They had planned to go to the Lake District, but two weeks before the wedding Tommy had an accident as he was driving along a dual carriageway on his way home from umpiring. 'I must have been dreaming,' he says 'and this car in front suddenly stopped. I swerved to miss him, but I hit the back of him.' Tommy was not badly injured, but the Hillman Husky was a write-off. 'So we'd no vehicle to go on honeymoon.' Plans were changed and a friend was able to motor the couple to Blackpool, where they had booked into a bed and breakfast in Palatine Road.

By the time they married, the business had done well enough for Tommy and Barbara to be able to put a deposit down for a small house in Bretherton not far from the cricket club and The Blue Anchor, still Tommy's local. A two-up, two-down terraced cottage built around the time of the Industrial Revolution, it would be their home for the next 36 years. On 29th May 1965, as their fourth wedding anniversary approached, their first daughter Hayley was born. Rather inconveniently she chose a Saturday to make her appearance, a day on which her father was umpiring at Leyland Motors. But all was well. 'As luck would have it the game ended at 5.20, so I was able to get to the hospital for the seven o'clock daddies' hour.'

Tommy had become keen to expand the business and he now made the crucial decision to take on the village newspaper round, shortly afterwards applying for a licence to sell alcohol. Supplying the papers each day meant that most of the villagers would have to come into the shop to settle their bills. The growth of supermarkets – the nearest to Bretherton is at Leyland, some five miles away – brought inevitable closure to most of the eight shops Tommy had known in his childhood, but becoming a general store with newspapers, greengroceries and drinks on sale ensured that Tommy and Barbara's was one that would survive, trading on as a traditional corner shop into the 1990s.

Hayley's arrival, just as they were taking on the newspaper round, prompted the young couple to change their car again. Though they had recently bought a Mini pickup, they now swapped it for a van where the baby's carry cot could be tucked safely behind the front seat as they travelled together to deliver the Sunday newspapers. With his cheery personality and love of meeting people, Tommy could have found few better ways of earning his living than running a village shop. It was certainly hard work and long hours. 'I often used to get up very early – two or three times a week in the summer to go to Preston market to buy strawberries. We used to sell a lot on a Saturday.' But being his own boss also ensured that he could manage to make time for his other interests. With an in-built love of serving others, he would soon become involved in a wide range of activities around the village, and when Saturday came round in the summer there would be no employer to hold him back as he indulged his passion for umpiring cricket. Had he passed the exam to become a railway booking clerk, it might have been a very different story!

Chapter Three

First steps on the umpiring ladder

Tommy's successful application to join the Southport & District League meant that the 15-year-old boy now had to make his own way to matches. With over 15 miles to travel to a club such as Skelmersdale, Tommy was sometimes able to use public transport, but more often he made the journey on his bicycle. 'I had a special bicycle with one pedal. It was a normal bike, but there was no pedal on the left-hand side. I could bat along with one leg and the other one hanging down.' Before long Tommy upgraded to a Schwinn with a small two-stroke engine driving the back wheel. Needing a mixture of petrol and oil, it proved a very economical machine to run, and it served Tommy well for several years. 'It was all right as long as I didn't drive through puddles. If you drove through a puddle, it wet the plug. You had just one plug and it used to splutter.'

For Tommy's first two seasons in the league, like all new umpires, he was confined to second division matches. In their third season umpires were assigned a mix of first and second division games, while there was a select cadre of officials who took only first division matches. Tommy eventually became one of this elite band, but before that, in 1957, he had already been chosen to take charge of the league's knock-out final. The weekly match fee when Tommy started earned him seven shillings and sixpence (37p), rising to ten shillings (50p) when he stood in first division matches. There was nothing extra for travel. Already it was the love of the game rather than any material reward that spurred him on. Keen to progress as an umpire and with favourable reports on his ability circulating, Tommy soon applied to join the panel of the more prestigious Lancashire League. He was still only 17 and he was turned down on the grounds of his age.

Aware of Tommy's growing reputation and ambition, a former minor counties umpire Arnold Crawshaw advised him that, if he wished to progress, he should apply to join the Northern League. Founded in controversial circumstances following a meeting at which clubs in the west of Lancashire had expressed themselves unhappy with the structure of the Ribblesdale League, the Northern League was formed in 1952. Over 50 years after Tommy joined its panel of umpires in 1962 it remains the league where he is still to be seen in action each summer despite efforts by the Lancashire League to lure him away once he had built up his reputation. 'I said no. You wouldn't have me when I was 17. You're not having me now!'

Over the years Tommy has seen many fine players in the Northern League and he reels off the names of some of the world stars: 'Javed Miandad, Malcolm Marshall, Gordon Greenidge, David Boon, Collie Smith, Franklin Stephenson and Jacques Kallis.' There have been many Lancashire players who have graduated from the league or returned to it when their playing days were over. Tommy mentions Jack Simmons and Bernard Reidy, but he picks Bob Entwistle as the most consistent batsman over the many years he has been associated with the league. Among bowlers he nominates another one-time Lancashire player Colin Hilton, along with David Halliwell, veteran of over 70 matches for Cumberland, as the fastest he has encountered. And he remembers a young Andrew Flintoff cutting his teeth with St Annes. Unswervingly loyal to the Northern League, Tommy became vice-chairman of its Umpires Association in 1978, taking over as chairman in 1984 and remaining in office ever since.

When Tommy began, the league played traditional timed cricket with declarations. 'Proper cricket – I liked timed cricket.' It later moved to 36 eight-ball overs a side then, after a spell of 110 overs, it has come in line with other leagues of comparable status in adopting a 50-over format. In the early days Tommy remembers that matches started much later – 2.30 instead of one o'clock – with a scheduled finish at 7.30 or 7.45 that could be put back if either side felt it had the chance of winning. 'If you had taken seven wickets, you could claim an extra five overs. And if you got within 30 runs batting second, you could also have an extra five overs. But once you'd claimed those overs, you had to play them. You might get beat! You had to weight it up.'

The later starting time made life easier when Tommy was busy with the shop. And there was none of the current practice of umpires arriving an hour in advance to ensure compliance with the laws of the game which now require them on the ground 45 minutes before the scheduled start and expect them to supervise the toss. 'Fifteen minutes if you were lucky!' Saturdays were usually busy in the shop, and they stayed open until eight o'clock with the arrival of the football pinks in the early days, though as the years passed they found that they could close a bit earlier. Especially as Barbara enjoyed coming to some of the more attractive venues, they relied on other family members and paid staff to assist. Tommy's mother, who lived until 1973, sometimes came down on her bike to help out. 'And we had a nephew of my brother who did Saturdays for a while.'

Where league panels now require umpires to have been trained and passed exams, those officiating in the 1950s learnt the job in the middle. Tommy had been fastidious in studying the laws, but it was not until the winter before the 1964 season that he attended a proper training course. No such courses had been available in the area until Major Ted Claridge ran one under the auspices of the embryo ACU. Tommy remains full of admiration for the major, whose classes provided him with a solid grounding in the skills of umpiring that he himself would pass on to future generations. 'He was a wonderful fellow, that Major Claridge. He ended as a Chelsea Pensioner.' 'It was the winter before Hayley was born,' Barbara recalls. 'I know I was pregnant at the time and we were driving over to Manchester once a week. I had a cousin living there and I'd drop Tommy off and stay with my cousin for a couple of hours and then pick him up.'

Although the training was available for those who sought it out, Tommy still reckons that few of those who umpired in the Northern League had any qualification. 'Of about 33 umpires on the list only 13 of those were qualified to do it. Twenty of them had never sat an exam, been on a course or anything.' Tommy was soon to obtain his formal qualification. A letter from the secretary of the Examination Board of the Northern branch of the ACU dated 6th June 1967 informed him that he had 'satisfied the ACU examiners in written and oral work.' His marks were 85% for the written exam and 86½% for the oral. The letter went on to advise him that 'for Full Membership a high standard of practical field work is necessary, and in this respect we shall be writing in early course to your nominated referees as to your experience and capabilities.' On 28th November that same year Tom Smith himself wrote to tell Tommy that he had been admitted to Full Membership. He was required to pay a subscription of 15 shillings (75p).

Tommy was now in a position to market himself as a fully qualified umpire and he wasted little time in advising Lancashire County Cricket Club of his availability. He was soon to be rewarded with a letter sent as far in advance as February inviting him to stand in an unusual match in aid of Ken Higgs' benefit fund: Manchester City v Manchester United to be played on Sunday 21st July, 1968. The match ultimately raised some £2,000 towards a benefit fund of around £8,500 for the Lancashire and England bowler. But it was not the jolly occasion for which everyone had hoped.

Twelve thousand spectators poured into Old Trafford to see the two sides, both replete with international stars, do battle. The benefit organisers came to see the umpires before the match started. They feared any incident that might spark trouble. 'The main one you mustn't give out,' they said, 'is George Best. So do something about it if he looks like being out.' Obscene chanting to greet the players taking the field did not bode well. The match got under way with City in the field, and the organisers made sure that

Best batted at the top of the order for United. 'He skied this ball,' Tommy remembers, 'and it looked as though it would be caught. So I immediately called no ball. Nobody knew that it wasn't a no ball, but it saved trouble at that stage.' Before long even the umpires couldn't save Best, but with one hero gone it was too much for the partisan crowd when Bobby Charlton was then bowled. The two sets of fans had not been segregated, and the rival clans went into battle. Windows were smashed and bottles flew. Though there was enough order for the match to be continued, the end came with a pitch invasion and the stumps ripped out of the ground. There were six arrests. Football hooliganism had come to a cricket ground. 'We will have to think twice before holding this sort of match,' said Jack Wood, secretary of the County Club, as the benefit organisers began to calculate how much of the money raised would have to be diverted to pay for the damage.

Tommy's overtures to Lancashire continued to bear fruit. He was soon invited to officiate at the county's pre-season friendlies, stepping up from 1972 to take charge of some Second Eleven matches. A Red Rose man through and through, a country member of the County Club for many years from 1969 and destined to become a life member of the Lancashire Cricket Board, it has always struck Tommy as curious that his first championship match should have involved his own county. Had he just retired from playing the first-class game, there would have been an interval of some years before being asked to stand in a match involving his old mates. Yet the frequency with which he was asked to umpire miscellaneous games at Old Trafford as well as matches in the Second Eleven Championship, where the home county was always responsible for appointing both umpires, ensured that those in the Lancashire dressing room for his Headingley debut would all have known him intimately.

He looks back and smiles at some of the memories. One of the first appointments came in 1970 when Lancashire played a 40-over friendly match against Cambridge University in early July to give the county team some practice ahead of their Gillette Cup quarter-final three days later. The University, captained by England rugby international and Essex pace bowler Tony Jorden, had one of its strongest sides for some years. There were players who would re-enter Tommy's life in the seasons ahead, Roger Knight, destined to captain Surrey, and Philip Carling, whom Tommy would encounter as chief executive of Nottinghamshire, but their outstanding player was Pakistan Test batsman Majid Khan, who had already passed a thousand first-class runs for the season. The University batted first and their 188 for 6 proved enough for a 74-run win, but the innings of their star batsman was a short one. Majid Khan had faced only a couple of balls from John Sullivan when one passed through to wicket-keeper Keith Goodwin. There was a loud appeal and, rather to Tommy's surprise, his colleague's finger went up. That colleague was a legendary figure from the umpiring world, Tommy Drinkwater, who had been on the first-class list in the early 1960s. Having heard no sound of bat on ball, Tommy walked over to Drinkwater at the fall of the next wicket. 'I said, "Majid Khan – that must have been a thin edge." "Yes," he said, "me and Goody and John Sullivan met up last night over a pint and we said we'd make sure he didn't make a big score." I was dumbfounded.' Until that moment Tommy had thought that Drinkwater's fame rested only on his having a false hand, the result of a Second World War accident. 'He once knocked in the stumps with this metal hand, hit them hard and the hand came off!' Tommy would soon enjoy further escapades with Drinkwater, a faithful Lancashire supporter invariably to be seen in his old age watching the cricket from beneath the old score box at the Stretford End.

Pre-season practice games at Old Trafford often had a touch of levity, and Tommy Wilson has always been an umpire who can enter into the spirit of the occasion. A traditional fixture was between a team of second team players and Cheshire. 'It was one of those occasions when we'd all get invited to go upstairs into the hierarchy bar and have a drink and a chat afterwards. For this game Cheshire had a keeper Tommy Hodson – he's still playing cricket now in his seventies. He had a bag with a draw string at the top, like you see with glasses cases. He said, "I've fetched this thing out. Would you mind putting it in your pocket?" It was a laughing box and it started laughing like you hear on the front at Blackpool. Ha, ha, ha… everybody fell about laughing. I pulled this thing out of my pocket. Tommy Hodson had tears coming down his face behind the stumps. I couldn't get it to stop. "Don't worry, Tommy. Put it in your pocket – it'll stop by magic." I put it back in my pocket and it stopped. The bowler set off on his run-up again and – it must have been timed – just as he enters his delivery stride this laughing box went off again. Three times it went off.' Eddie Slinger, captain of Lancashire Second Eleven, was batting. 'He wasn't amused. "Tommy, it's not cricket. Turn the damn thing off." But I couldn't do it.'

Edwin Slinger, later to become a distinguished circuit judge, was a man Tommy greatly respected, not least for his insistence that those who played under him should walk if they knew they were out. He was also one of those to whom Tommy turned in the autumn of 1968 when he decided to apply to join the list of minor counties umpires. Another from whom Tommy asked for a few kind words was Joe Blackledge, who had led Lancashire for the single season of 1962, the swansong for the amateur in English county cricket. Blackledge lived at Croston, a village close to Bretherton, and Tommy remembers going round to his home and helping him compose his response to MCC's request for a reference. They must have said the right things. Within days of Blackledge writing, a letter arrived at the Bretherton shop from S.C. Griffith, secretary of MCC, informing Tommy that he would be on the reserve list for 1969. The letter explained that should anyone should drop off the list or if there were difficulties in covering a particular match, Tommy might be called upon.

Despite his aspirations to umpire cricket at a higher level, Tommy remained involved with the running of the Southport & District League and never lost interest in his local Bretherton club. The local paper was able to report that he was in the chair when 54 sat down for the club's annual dinner and presentations at The Blue Anchor, at which they were able to celebrate Bretherton's return to the first division of the league for the 1969 season. The AGM saw Tommy re-elected as chairman as the meeting dealt with the minutiae essential to the running of any small club. A loss of approximately £30 on the season had been due to the complete overhaul of the mower, while the increasing number of lady spectators had prompted the club to improve the toilet facilities for them.

Joe Blackledge

Chapter Four

Accepted for the minor counties

In mid-February 1969 Tommy received a letter from Lord's. It came on MCC headed writing paper. Though D.B. Carr, with J.G. Dunbar and J.A. Bailey, was one of three assistant secretaries listed beneath the letterhead, Donald Carr's signature at the bottom of the letter was above a new title – Assistant Secretary TCCB. This was the moment of departure when MCC was surrendering responsibility for the governance of the domestic game. However, with Billy Griffith secretary of both organisations and with both housed in the Lord's pavilion, early TCCB committees appeared to be little more than old MCC faces recycled under new hats and, it would appear, the new body was using up old MCC stationery. It will have mattered little to Tommy, for the letter brought the important news that he had been appointed to umpire two matches in what was then styled the County Championship – 2nd Division. In common parlance it was still the Minor Counties.

Carr's letter told Tommy that he would be required at Bramhall on Wednesday, 28th May to umpire Cheshire v Lancashire Second Eleven and that he would also be in charge when Shropshire met Cambridgeshire at Shrewsbury in mid-June. Enclosed with the letter were the terms of his engagement and a pre-stamped and addressed post card back to Lord's that he was required to sign confirming that he agreed 'not to write for the Press etc.' The same restrictions apply in modern times, now extended to include social media.

For his first match in minor counties cricket Tommy was given an experienced colleague. Les Hoff had seven seasons behind him on the list and was a man well equipped to help Tommy through any initial problems. A railway worker, for whom this was to be his last summer of minor counties cricket, Hoff continued to umpire in the North Staffordshire and Cheshire League for many more years and Tommy met him on later occasions watching Cheshire or Staffordshire play.

'A wonderful experience' is the caption in Tommy's scrap book beneath the scorecard of his first minor counties match. Rain delayed the start, and the pitch was never easy for batsmen. Winning the toss, Lancashire Seconds batted first and declared at 101 for 8 with Barry Wood contributing 52. Two of the giants of Cheshire cricket, captain Freddie Millett and a later long-term skipper Arthur Sutton, shared the eight wickets that fell. Cheshire declared early on the second day with four wickets down as soon as the Lancashire score had been passed, Millett top scoring with 39 not out. Wood, normally a first team player for whom the match represented a return to action after a domestic accident suffered in trying to build a garage, dominated again with 89 from a total of 201 for six as Lancashire set up the kind of challenge on which two-day minor county cricket thrived. Sutton made 45, but so little support did he receive that Cheshire slumped to 62 all out.

The hero for Lancashire was leg spinner Derek Parker, whose seven wickets all fell to catches at a cost of just ten runs. Curiously Parker, who played 77 second team matches for Lancashire, never made a first-class appearance. He played briefly as professional for Leyland Motors, only a few miles from Bretherton, before moving to Durham, where Tommy remembers meeting him again. 'He was wearing a huge gold cross. He'd taken to religion, very much so. But they were rare, proper leg spinners. It's a pity he didn't go on to play first-class cricket.' Parker found greater fame in later life as a novelist. Among his works was 'The Pained Willow', a semi-autographical story of a league professional in the north of England, published shortly before his death in 2013.

At Shrewsbury Tommy stood with one of three namesakes on the list, Roddy Wilson from the Midlands. As if four Wilsons were not enough, with Tommy and Roddy the potential for muddle in the records – and in the memories of those taking part in matches – was the greater for the pair suffering a common walking disability. In fact, Tommy believes Roddy was the more severely afflicted. 'It affected both his legs. He went on the field with a walking stick. I've known him go out with two sticks.' Like Tommy, Roddy enjoyed a long and distinguished career in minor counties cricket. His marks in the championship brought him a string of appointments to the minor counties' annual match with the touring team, and would also gain him admission to the first-class list. Some years later he would be involved with Tommy and others in setting up a Minor Counties Umpires Association. Tommy remembers that Roddy, seven years his senior, eventually had to give up all umpiring because he found his hands were affected through constantly having to put weight on his arm crutches.

The match at Shrewsbury opened unhappily for Cambridgeshire, whose captain and opening batsman David Fairey was injured early in the game when he had scored only 8 and could take no further part. After Shropshire declared with a lead of 98, the visitors, with Fairey unable to bat, could muster only 178. This left Shropshire a target of 81 for victory. But the clock was against them as they managed only 58 for three before time ran out.

Reports from the two matches in which he stood in 1969 must have served Tommy well. When the captains met to choose the umpires for the following season, he was appointed to the full list. The news was received enthusiastically by the local papers, a posed picture acting as a reminder that this was still the era of long white coats and umpires who bent low at the bowler's end. 'Once upon a time,' the latest edition of Tom Smith's concedes, 'it was thought advisable for the umpire to bend forward during the time of the bowler's run-up and delivery.' Despite recent Hawkeye tests suggesting that umpires give more accurate decisions when seated on a chair than when standing upright, other factors, notably the need for mobility, have led to a text-book preference for the upright stance. 'Yes,' says Tommy, 'when I started umpiring, I put my left leg behind me, right leg in front and I used to umpire like that. My eyes were just above the level of the stumps. That's the way I used to umpire. Unbelievable really!'

Mr. Thomas Guy Wilson, of South Road, Bretherton (pictured above), has been appointed by the M.C.C. to the list of reserve umpires for the minor county matches during the coming season. Chairman of Bretherton Cricket Club, he was recently elected to the executive committee of the Southport and District Amateur Cricket League.

Southport Visiter
18 January 1969

The official letter telling Tommy of his appointment was soon followed by another allotting him eight matches. The desire to restrict umpires' travelling meant that all would be in the northern half of the country, Wolverhampton being the furthest south he would need to travel. He would remain an umpire on the Minor Counties Cricket Association (MCCA) list without a break until the end of the 2002 season, thereafter returning for just one match in 2004. The letter of appointment from S.C. Griffith spelled out the terms on which he would be recompensed for his duties:

> The fees for the 1970 season will be £10. 0s. 0d. per match, plus second-class railway fares and a nightly allowance, properly vouched, up to a maximum of £3. 0s. 0d. to cover lodging expenses. The nightly allowance will not be paid for nights on which an Umpire is not required to live away from his home though, in such cases, train or bus fares may be paid instead, for each day of travelling.
>
> Where an Umpire returns home at the conclusion of a match, he will not be entitled to claim a night allowance to cover part of his journey home, unless he can establish that he could not have reached his home by midnight of that day. If he cannot reach his home by midnight, then the Ground Authority of the ground on which he has been officiating will be required to pay a night allowance up to a maximum of £3. 0s. 0d., and as properly vouched.

A feature of the system which Tommy would also encounter in the first-class game was that the match fee was paid centrally while other expenses were claimed from the home county, quaintly referred to as the Ground Authority in Billy Griffith's letter. The matter of expenses prompts Ken Shenton, appointed to the list in 1984, to recall the first time he and Tommy umpired together, at Leek in Staffordshire. Living in Blackpool, where he was a teacher of classical music at Arnold School, he would have travelled from the seaside town to reach the match.

'Breezy is it in Blackpool?' Ken well remembers the opening remark of Laurance Hancock, Staffordshire's long-serving secretary, when he and Tommy presented themselves at the ground. Tommy explains the gibe: 'We claimed two nights and he felt we should only have claimed one and gone down in the morning.' For a journey approaching 90 miles with a driving time estimated at one hour 42 minutes in trouble-free conditions on today's roads, it might be thought that the two umpires had made a sensible decision in travelling the night before to make sure of arriving fresh and in good time for a six or seven hour stint on the field. Arguably it would have been irresponsible to risk the morning traffic. But this was not how Hancock saw it. 'Laurance was always quite tight.'

Among the northern umpires with whom he has stood in MCCA matches none stands higher in Tommy's estimation than Ken Shenton, but none provided him with more amusement than Tommy Drinkwater, the Captain Hook of umpiring, who sometimes wore a false hand but on other occasions favoured a hook. Tommy recalls officiating with Drinkwater at Alderley Edge in Cheshire. They were sitting together at lunch with Tommy giving his partner a hand in cutting up his food. He noticed Drinkwater eyeing up some huge cheeses in the middle of the table. 'We had just finished lunch, when Tommy whispered in my ear, "Is nobody going to eat that cheese? Have you got a paper bag in your pocket?" I said "No," whereupon his hand with a hook shot forward and stabbed the biggest cheese and dropped it on my plate! "Put it in your pocket – it'll last me all week!"'

That evening, as they shared a few pints, Drinkwater enquired what arrangements Tommy had made for the night. The three pound allowance was not enough to find a bed in opulent Alderley Edge and Tommy had to admit that he was would be paying a fiver. He left to go to his hotel, returning early next morning to supervise the mowing of the pitch, as the regulations required. 'I went to find the groundsman who told me it had been cut. "Your mate watched me do it," he said. I was amazed because Tommy usually arrived later than me. I went into the pavilion looking for him only to find him behind the steel grill of the bar stood in a string vest having a wash in the sink with his false hand on the bar top. I asked where he had spent the night and he told me he'd slept on the seats in the lounge bar!' So much for the 'properly vouched' expense claims stipulated in Mr Griffith's letter!

Tommy was now entering a time when he could expect at least half a dozen MCCA games most years, while he was also getting regular appointments from Lancashire to stand in their second eleven matches. In 1972 he was scheduled to officiate at Harrogate for a second team match between Yorkshire and Lancashire. On this occasion it was in the Minor Counties Championship, in which, with Somerset, they were the only first-class counties still choosing to compete. Before the match there was a letter for Tommy from S.C. Griffith at Lord's. It told him that Geoff Cope, Yorkshire's off spinner, would be appearing for the home county after a spell away from the game following suspension on account of his action. 'Yorkshire were told,' Griffith wrote, 'that as soon as they considered his action had improved sufficiently they should play him in one or two Second XI matches.' Tommy was asked for comments when he sent in his report on the match.

Geoff Cope would later play three Test matches for England, but he had had a tough introduction to the game. Playing first under Brian Close, he had been encouraged to look to take wickets, but following Close's departure and the disintegration of a once strong Yorkshire side, containment had been the principal requirement of his new captain, Geoff Boycott. Meanwhile there had been constant whispers that all was not well with his action. In 1972 came the ban. 'It was a bad time because you were never allowed to defend yourself,' Cope said later. 'A committee met and made a decision, which was then passed on down the lines. You didn't know who was on that committee or what they thought. But Dickie Bird and a lot of other people have said "Geoff, there's nothing wrong; if you were guilty, then an awful lot of others were."' Determined to put matters right, Cope had received extensive help from the former Test left-armer Johnny Wardle and had re-modelled his action to bring his arm from behind his back, much as Wardle himself had done. In the process he had found himself once again an attacking bowler. 'When I'd got my arm behind the back, the left shoulder would come round more and I ended up in an up-and-over action and got a bit more bounce from it and was able to underspin it if I wished.'

There have always been differences of opinion with suspect actions and there would be complaints again later in Cope's career, but there was a challenge facing Tommy and his fellow umpire, Tommy Drinkwater. Sadly there was all too little on which they could report. Lancashire reached 95 for five on a rain-affected first day, after which the players never returned to the field. Cope had bowled three overs for two runs without any eyebrows raised over his action. It fell to Tommy, at square leg, to pass official comment and in his report to Billy Griffith he was able to say that he saw nothing wrong.

Had there been any serious doubts about the legitimacy of Cope's action, Tommy would not have shirked carrying out his duty. A few weeks later there was to be match in which the issue of a suspect delivery action would cause Tommy fresh doubts. Northumberland were playing Cheshire at Neston. In the Northumberland side was their West Indian professional Clairmonte Depeiaza. Back in April 1955, in the series against Australia, Depeiaza had won Test caps as a wicket-keeper. In the fourth Test at Bridgetown, he had joined his captain Dennis Atkinson in the most desperate of situations. Australia had made 668, and the scoreboard read 147 for six as Depeiaza made his way to the crease. He and Atkinson then added 347, still a world record for the seventh wicket in all Test cricket. It helped to earn West Indies a draw, but it was to be Depeiaza's only first-class century in a career that brought him fewer than a thousand runs.

That winter he went to New Zealand with an experimental West Indies side in which he and Alfred Binns, both with some aspirations as batsmen, would share the wicket-keeping duties. Neither player had a distinguished tour, but both were selected for the first Test, Binns taking the gloves. West Indies were heavily reliant on the spin of Alf Valentine and Sonny Ramadhin, supplemented by the teenaged Garry Sobers, who had still to develop his fast-bowling skills, while the pace attack, apart from skipper Atkinson's medium-paced cutters, relied almost entirely on Frank King. When King broke down early on the first day, the captain summoned up Depeiaza for his first ever bowl in a first-class game. He had turned his arm for five overs in a two-day country match a few days earlier, and he now delivered three overs in the first innings and two in the second. Though neither umpire chose to call him, it appears that there were concerns about the part-time bowler's action. He never delivered another first-class ball, reverting to keeping wicket for what was to be his final Test before making way for Binns in the last two matches of the New Zealand series.

By 1972, Clairmonte Depeiaza, now 43, had found his way to Northumberland via a spell in the Lancashire League – and his strong suit now was his bowling! Though Cheshire won the match at Neston by four wickets, they had been skittled out for 120 in their first innings, with Depeiaza taking seven for 41. This was the West Indian's best return for Northumberland, but his action that day had aroused Tommy's curiosity – he was not satisfied as to its legality. 'It was virtually underarm bowling,' he says in trying to demonstrate the way Depeiaza brought his arm over. With none of the protocols now circulating throughout domestic cricket on doubtful actions, Tommy still chose not to call the bowler but wrote instead to the MCCA secretary. This was Laurance Hancock, the man who ruled for decades at Staffordshire. 'In my opinion Depeiaza throws it,' Tommy wrote, to which Hancock replied asking Tommy what he was going to do about it.

A few weeks later Tommy was umpiring Northumberland again, in their match against Staffordshire at Jesmond. His colleague was Brian Harrison, a bluff Yorkshireman renowned as a strong umpire and one for whom Tommy had great respect. 'He was a legend in his own lifetime, a big pal of Doug Padgett. He always talked to me as the senior umpire: "You leave it to me." He was a bit bombastic.' Before Northumberland took the field Tommy had a word with Harrison. 'I said "Watch Depeiaza. See what you think. Just watch him."' Harrison took up his position at the striker's end. Tommy did not have long to wait. After just three balls Harrison had made his mind up: 'No ball. He threw it!'

Tommy picks up the tale: 'Instead of the captain having a go at Brian, he swung round and came to me. "Wilson, that's your doing. I know you reported Clairmonte the other week at Cheshire. And you've told Harrison he throws. And Harrison's called him." I said, "No, I didn't tell Harrison he threw. I told him to have a look at him." Anyway he comes on at Harrison's end, so I thought there's nothing I can do but call him. So I called him.' Depeiaza lingered on in the Northumberland League, but his career in minor counties cricket had ended.

It was not the last time Tommy would have cause to question a bowler's action. Five years later he called a second Test player. David O'Sullivan had played for two seasons as a left-arm spinner with Hampshire. In his second, 1973, his 47 wickets at just over 20 each had helped his county win the Championship. O'Sullivan had already won the first of his 11 Test caps, but at the end of the season Hampshire decided to release him in favour of Andy Roberts, the West Indian fast bowler, as their overseas player.

Roberts had enjoyed great success in second eleven cricket that summer, but was still to win his first Test cap. He would eventually take 202 Test wickets at 25.61 and O'Sullivan only 18 at 67.83, but in 1973 it was not the obvious decision for Hampshire made so patent by hindsight. With no first-class contract for 1974, O'Sullivan joined Durham, for whom he played 39 championship matches over the next four years. With 174 wickets at less than 16 apiece, he became an integral part of the attack of one of the stronger minor counties.

Having no doubts that O'Sullivan's action was illegal, Tommy called him at Stockton-on-Tees in the match against Staffordshire. 'Are you convinced?' he was asked by Durham captain, Brian Lander. Assured that Tommy was quite certain, Lander admitted that his county had privately questioned their overseas bowler's mode of delivery. Tommy's subsequent enquiries revealed that other English umpires had also registered their doubts, and his suspect action had contributed to O'Sullivan's release from Hampshire. None of this prevented O'Sullivan from venting his spleen. 'You're out of order,' he told Tommy, 'I've played Test cricket all over the world and I haven't been called.' Tommy stood his ground: 'I told him to his face, "You throw."' O'Sullivan continued to play cricket overseas for another eight years, but after Tommy had called him at the end of the 1977 season he never played again in England, while in Christopher Martin-Jenkins' Who's Who of Test Cricketers 'a slight kink in his action' was identified as a reason why he was not selected for more Tests. Not for the last time had Tommy been prepared to tackle one of the game's thorniest issues.

The match at Jesmond with the Depeiaza incident was to be the last for Tommy in the 1972 season. Ill health forced him to withdraw from his last two MCCA appointments, and there were reports that he had suffered a heart attack. Complaining of breathlessness, he had been rushed to his local hospital, where an angina attack was diagnosed. Pills were prescribed, but Barbara was concerned that the medics had not got to the root of the problem. Prompted to visit a heart specialist in Preston, at a cost of £9, Tommy underwent a thorough examination. No scar tissue, the crucial indicator of a heart attack, was discovered and the specialist declared that Tommy had not had a heart attack nor was angina the problem. His diagnosis was that Tommy had been suffering from anxiety and had had a nervous breakdown. Asked what had been worrying him, Tommy had no doubts – the after effects of decimalisation, which had been introduced 18 months earlier. Though he had been on a course to prepare for the transition of the currency, the change had been a constant source of stress in the running of his small business.

Tommy was passed on to another specialist who dealt with mental disorders. The man he saw told him that he ran classes and he said that, if Tommy were to be cured of his problems, he should attend. Tommy went only twice. He found himself sitting among severely retarded people, mostly sitting slumped and unwilling or unable to communicate with the outside world. 'I thought: what am I doing in a place like this?' After the second visit, he returned home and said to Barbara, 'That's it. I'm not going again. I'm going to cure myself.' He had also been prescribed barbiturates and they had been making him feel peculiar. 'In my own mind I could walk up walls and walk across the ceiling. So I thought they're no good, so I kicked them into touch. And in a matter of months I was right as rain.'

There were sympathetic letters from Lord's as Tommy was obliged to withdraw from his last two minor counties appointments. Among other letters from friends was one from Jimmy Halliwell, the chairman of the Northern League Umpires Federation, who had written with a timely homily: 'Let this be a message in disguise, and do – and I mean do!! – cut out some of your activities.' Never an easy message for Tommy to obey!

Chapter Five

A place on the reserve list

Tommy's rise to the first-class umpires list was no accident. As early as 1971, after just two full seasons on the MCCA panel, he had submitted a formal application to Lord's. The reply from Donald Carr, by now on TCCB letterhead, still bore the formality of MCC's annual letter to minor counties umpires. 'Dear Sir' was the universal opening, the complementary signing off 'Yours faithfully'. Traditional courtesies were observed in the language: 'I regret to inform you that you were not amongst those selected.'

In 1975 Tommy's persistence paid off. With the retirement of Billy Griffith, Donald Carr had become secretary of the TCCB while Jack Bailey held a similar position with MCC. The two bodies were now to lead more separate lives, and as time passed their respective secretaries, once good friends, would increasingly be at loggerheads over such matters as corporate rights for Test matches at Lord's. In later life Tommy would also taste the politics of the game's administration, but there were no such thoughts as he opened the letter and found not the customary polite rejection but news that 'at their recent meeting, the Umpires Sub-Committee appointed you to the reserve list of First-Class umpires for the 1976 season.' Tommy had broken through into the freemasonry of first-class cricket, his place tacitly acknowledged when Donald Carr's letter the following April, enclosing a cheque for £50 as a 'retainer' (TCCB's inverted commas), bore the salutation 'Dear Mr Wilson', and was signed off with the less austere 'Yours sincerely'.

There had originally been no guarantee of any appointments, but Laurie Gray, recalled as a reserve after two years off the main list, had been unable to take up his appointment, so Tommy was given just one match – a Gillette Cup first round game at Hitchin, where Hertfordshire were to play Berkshire on Saturday 26th June. His colleague was to be David Evans, whose telephone number was supplied along with regulations for the knock-out competition. Little did Tommy know that Evans' indisposition earlier in the season would bring him a higher-profile debut in the Roses match. 'Very nice bloke' says Tommy of the former Glamorgan wicket-keeper, 'but he was a bit frail and he worried a lot about not getting work in the winter. He said you can't manage on what the umpires get unless you can get a job in the winter.'

The match at Hitchin was played on one of the very hottest days in what had been a scorching summer. So hot was it that the umpires removed their coats, behaviour that was considered newsworthy back in 1976. Tommy remembers it vividly. 'There wasn't a blade of grass on the outfield – it was completely brown. And they took drinks every half hour. They were brought in buckets of iced water with plastic cups.' Put in to bat, Berkshire made 158 for eight in their 50 overs. After losing four wickets for 21, they were indebted to a fifth wicket stand of 95 between their opening batsman David Johnston, the son of England footballer Harry Johnston, who top-scored with 68, and their captain Michael Mence, once of Warwickshire, who made 44. When Hertfordshire were 76 for six, Berkshire's score looked to be enough, but their captain, wicket-keeper Frank Collyer, who was to be a mainstay of the side for 21 summers, rose to the challenge. With Stuart Ambrose he added 59, enabling Herts to squeeze home by two wickets. Man of the Match was their opening bowler Brian Collins, whose five for 20 included three of the early wickets.

Tommy was to see Hertfordshire again at the end of the season. He had been allocated his usual share of minor counties matches and on 3rd September came a letter from Donald Carr informing him that he had been chosen to stand in the Minor Counties Challenge Match at Chester-le-Street. This was the match in which the second team in the table, Hertfordshire on this occasion, was enabled to challenge the county that had finished top. It was the first time Tommy had been selected for this prestigious three-day game, which carried the same fee, £18 plus expenses, as paid for standing in MCCA's tourist match. In the end he and Stan Levison were paid for watching the rain. Not a ball was bowled until the third day when Durham reached 100 for five in 42 overs.

Tommy remembers Jack Iley, Durham's secretary, had champagne on ice ready for celebrations after the game. 'He wasn't known as a generous man,' Tommy says, 'but he had this champagne and he said, "Come on, you umpires, have a glass of champagne. They haven't won it, they haven't won it!"' Durham were indeed the champions because the challengers had been denied the chance to knock them off the perch. Iley would no doubt have preferred his side to have taken the field and won, but they had taken the title nonetheless.

Tommy's second year on the reserve list brought him four first-class matches. He began with two season-openers in The Parks at Oxford, where the University played first Warwickshire and then Worcestershire. His colleague for both games was John Langridge, a popular umpire with seven Tests to his credit who had been allowed to stay on the list beyond the customary retiring age. 'A big tall fellow, he used to stoop down to umpire – the old brigade.' Of all the first-class umpires with whom Tommy was to stand, John Langridge remained his firm favourite. 'He was a marvellous help to me.'

Early season pitches shaped both matches, with the April weather keeping the players in the pavilion for long periods. There was a blank opening day in the first match, after which Oxford, captained by Vic Marks, began well with an opening stand of 86 before subsiding to 153 all out. Warwickshire, having lost Dennis Amiss for a duck, slumped to 53 for four before Neal Abberley's 55 enabled them to reach 187. In seaming conditions where Marks chose not to give his off-breaks a single over, it was the tall David Gurr who took the eye with five for 42. Two years later this promising quick bowler, who had joined Somerset, would lose all semblance of rhythm and control and slip out of the game for good. The county's slender lead was nevertheless a platform for victory as the University, in their second knock, mustered only 59, Warwickshire cruising to victory by eight wickets.

Worcestershire's Jim Cumbes was the next to enjoy the April dampness with six for 40, his captain Norman Gifford sending down only four overs of spin as the University were bundled out for 158, with rain again foreshortening the first day's play. There was time for Basil D'Oliveira to score 84 in Worcestershire's reply of 185 for six before the weather claimed the final day

Tommy's next match takes second place only to his Roses debut at Headingley as he looks back on the highlights of his career as a first-class umpire. Cec Pepper had been scheduled to stand in Northants' match against the Australian touring team, and when he had to withdraw, Tommy stepped in. His colleague at Northampton was Jack van Geloven, a man whom he had umpired when he was playing for Northumberland. Played in mid-July, the Northants match came between the second and third Tests. To Tommy's disappointment neither Dennis Lillee nor Jeff Thomson was playing but, with Australia one down in the series, several of the tourists had the chance to make a mark and win a place in the Test side.

Greg Chappell won the toss and, with an undefeated 161, treated the Saturday crowd to one of the finest exhibitions of batting they could hope to see. A declaration well before the close at 328 for six failed to bring the tourists an early wicket, but the next day belonged to Lennie Pascoe. Operating from Tommy's end, he troubled all the Northants batsmen with his pace. Finishing with six for 68, he had bowled himself back into the Test side for Trent Bridge. There were 16 no balls in the innings total of 236, seven of them bowled by Pascoe and called by Tommy, one when he was on a hat-trick. When the Australians batted a second time, Chappell delayed his declaration in favour of batting practice, a target of 331 in 220 minutes leaving Northants with only a draw to play for, which they achieved for the loss of only one wicket.

Bishen Bedi bowling to Greg Chappell

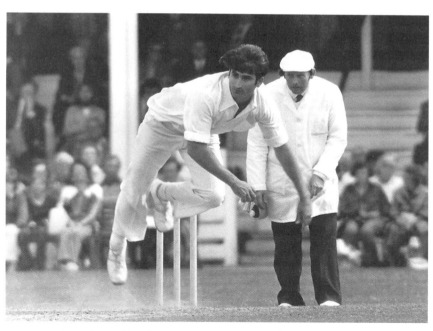

Len Pascoe bowling as Tommy watches for another no ball

With the match fizzling out as a contest, a press headline made the most of 'some verbals' between David Hookes and Peter Willey. Hookes had been batting tentatively until goaded into a burst of ferocious hitting, twice lifting Willey over the rope. However, the Northants man got his revenge a few minutes later when he clean bowled Hookes, sending the Australian on his way with a 'two handed Harvey Smith gesture.' In Tommy's judgement it wasn't the big issue the reporter was painting it, and it was dealt with before it had the chance to escalate further.

There was better humour as the final stages of a moribund match were enlivened by left-arm spinner Ray Bright imitating Bishen Bedi, Northants' Indian Test bowler. Bedi was party to the deception as the already bearded Ray Bright took the field with a darkened face and wearing a Sikh patka. Coming on to bowl, he then gave a perfect imitation of the Indian's action. 'The crowd thought, what's Bedi doing on the field for Australia,' says Tommy. 'He was the spitting image of Bedi.' The one wicket to fall had gone to Bright. Or was it Bedi? 'There was little else to smile at' was the laconic comment of John Mason writing in The Daily Telegraph.

Always one to collect stories for after-dinner entertainment, Tommy relates one he picked up at Northampton. Peter Watts, the county's leg spinner, was playing in one of the popular Cavaliers matches that took place on Sundays in the days before the John Player League. Watts was bowling with Irish umpire Ron Odell standing at his end as Tommy picks up the story. 'He hits the pads. "How's that?" "Not out." Well this happened three times. So Peter pulled out his wallet and gave Ron a pound note. Ron says, "Do I take this as a bribe?" "No," says Peter, "buy your guide dog some biscuits." But that's not the end of the story. Peter comes out to bat. First ball – bang on the pad. Peter thought, no way, he can't give me out. He looked down the pitch at Ron with a sigh of relief. Ron was looking down. "What do you think, Rover?" Then he lifts his head. "Yes!" And he puts his finger up!'

On the Sunday of the Australian match Tommy and van Geloven had made the short journey from Northampton to Milton Keynes, where Northants were to play their JPL match against Yorkshire on the Manor Fields ground. It proved to be one of those games where the rain gods mock anyone seen in white flannels. Yorkshire made a disastrous start with Geoff Boycott caught behind in the first over. Restricted by mid-innings rain to 36 overs, they reached 166 for seven. The Northants reply was terminated when they had scored 40 without loss off 6.3 overs. Had they reached 47 off the next 21 balls, they would have had the superior run rate at the crucial ten-over mark, but a final surge of rain meant that both teams left with two points each. With both sides near the bottom of the table, little was at stake, allowing the two umpires to abandon the game without recrimination.

There was one final match for Tommy, when he deputised for Dickie Bird, teaming up with Arthur Jepson at Wellingborough School for Northants' championship match with Middlesex, into which would be sandwiched a 40-over JPL game on the same ground against Essex . The start to the championship match was delayed by morning rain. A capricious pitch then gave the spinners control of the match. Middlesex, champions in 1976, were making a strong challenge to retain their title and, on winning the toss, asked the home team to bat. For a while Northants prospered. With Geoff Cook making 83, they reached 160 for three before John Emburey and Phil Edmonds made the most of the conditions to restrict the score to 179.

However, with three Middlesex wickets falling before the close for just 18, the day ended with Northants strongly placed. It was a foretaste of what was to come when play resumed on the Monday. With Bedi and Willey taking five wickets each, Middlesex capsized for 62. There was only one over of pace before Emburey and Edmonds were back at work, but Northants reached 217 to set a formidable last innings target. Middlesex were not up to the task, losing by 128 runs as Bedi ended with match figures of eleven for 107.

To some this might appear to have been a good old-fashioned contest on an outground with help for the spinners from an uncovered pitch. But the match had been marred by poor groundsmanship with embarrassment on the first day when it was discovered that the stumps were pitched so incompetently that a ball would have been able to pass through without disturbing a bail. The umpires decided the pitch should be reported to the TCCB. 'It just wasn't good enough for county cricket,' Tommy says. 'It was turning absolutely square. It was so bad the spinners were opening with the new ball.' The report went in, but this was long before pitch inspectors were appointed to rush round as soon as wickets were tumbling too freely, and Tommy heard no more of the matter.

Chapter Six

Trousers from Burton's for a first-class umpire

The summer of 1978 was the one in which Tommy was elevated to the full first-class panel. The formal contract running to four pages was drawn up in the language that enriches lawyers: 'WHEREAS the selection of First-Class umpire is made by T.C.C.B. and T.C.C.B. has now approved the appointment of the Umpire............' The original plan had been that Tommy should do only half a season, so the standard document was amended to acknowledge that his employment would run from 1st July to 8th September. For this he was to be paid £1,500 in three monthly instalments. For any appointments over and above those allocated to him there would be a further £50 for a three-day match and £20 if standing for one day. Tommy's eyes may have glazed over at the paragraph setting out that, should he be called up for a Test match, he would receive £750. Reasonable expenses would be reimbursed. A separate letter confirmed the overnight allowance at £14, while rising fuel costs lifted the umpires' mileage rate from 10p to 12p per mile. By comparison, those officiating in the Minor Counties Championship in the same season were receiving only £15 per two-day match with a nightly allowance of £8. First-class status also carried with it the right to charge first-class rail fares – but no taxis!

The half-season arrangement for Tommy came about because this was a time when the TCCB invited leading overseas umpires to officiate in the English summer. In 1977 Tom Brooks of Australia and the West Indian Douglas Sang Hue had stood. They had found working a full season an uncomfortably long time to be away from home; so for 1978, when Sathyaji Rao from India and New Zealander Fred Goodall joined the panel, it was for only the first half of the summer. Tommy was originally allocated ten championship matches and nine one-day contests, seven in the John Player League and two in the Gillette Cup. However, in late May Barrie Meyer was rushed to hospital with a duodenal ulcer. This meant he was out of cricket umpiring until July, so Tommy was drafted in to take over his matches. 'Does that include the Test?' he asked more in jest than hope. He was to learn that it did not even take in the Varsity Match, where Roddy Wilson, also on the full panel for the first time, had already been chosen. Such was still the perceived importance of this fixture that Brian Langley was constrained to write that TCCB did not feel it right for two 'part season' umpires to stand. Bill Alley would be at Lord's instead, with Tommy taking his place for the Surrey v Kent game at The Oval.

Hitherto Tommy had had to find his own umpiring coat and trousers, but the first-class panel were better provided for. Cec Pepper had picked up a contract to supply coats – two per umpire – though Tommy's recollection is that he didn't qualify for one. However, he took advantage of the chance to acquire some trousers. 'You got money for trousers. You could go to any Burton's shop and they measured you up. You filled in a form and they billed TCCB. It was usually two pairs, but I was doing half a season so they only gave me one pair!'

One match came Tommy's way before he began filling the gap left by Meyer. He received a call from Lord's one morning: 'Can you go down to Edgbaston?' One of the umpires had been taken ill, by coincidence David Evans, whose earlier indisposition had given Tommy his debut match at Headingley two years earlier. Tommy immediately agreed, but he had over 100 miles to travel. 'Don't worry, get there when you can,' said Brian Langley. When he arrived, he found David Constant standing at both ends while Alan Oakman, Warwickshire's coach, was at square leg. Warwickshire were batting and Dennis Amiss was making the most of a good pitch on his way to a century. Those watching had wondered at his headgear. In the days before anything had been designed to protect a batsman's head, he had worn what Michael Melford described as 'an American football-type' helmet. The Daily Telegraph's correspondent went on to express the view that it was 'three feet too high for the bounce of the ball on this placid pitch.'

At 307 for four the Warwickshire innings ended, the regulations under which matches were played bringing an enforced closure after 100 overs. In those days spectators got more play for their money, and an hour was left for Geoff Boycott to lay the foundation for what would become his 104th century the next day. Boycott had learned that day that he was not to retain the England captaincy that he had assumed in New Zealand after an injury to Mike Brearley. Not arriving in time for the pre-match formalities, Tommy had still to be introduced to the great man. He did not have long to wait. 'In my first over, Willis was bowling and shouted for lbw against Boycott, who was playing a shot only just outside off stump. I said "Not Out". They ran a leg bye and when he arrived at my end he said, "Geoff Boycott, good to meet you. That was a good decision. I am on the umpires subcommittee, you know."' Boycott's innings next day was a slow affair, but with John Hampshire and Kevin Sharp accelerating, Yorkshire, also obliged to close after 100 overs, finished on 302 for six. The loss of four Warwickshire wickets overnight for 84 promised an interesting final day.

So it proved, though when Warwickshire were all out setting a target of only 145, few thought it would be beyond Yorkshire. However, overnight rain had added life to the uncovered pitch and Warwickshire's attack was spearheaded by Bob Willis with an ever-willing David Brown in support. Tommy recalls Willis as one of the gentlemen of the circuit, accepting decisions without demur, but the speed of his bowling in this match now tested the umpire's reactions. 'He came thundering in and bowled the ball. I lifted my head up and the wicket-keeper was just taking it.' This was part of Tommy's education in the first-class game, where the speed of what happens can take a novice umpire unawares. Tommy now sees it as imperative for an umpire to move only his eyes, never his head, but not then. 'Nobody had told me any different. I learnt from that day onwards – no movement of the head.' Willis took three wickets that day, but it was the 36 year-old Brown, with five for 53 in an unbroken spell of 21 overs, who sealed a remarkable 34-run victory for Warwickshire as Yorkshire were bowled out for 110.

Warwickshire were to enjoy Tommy's company in his next match, when he was at Worcester with Lloyd Budd as his colleague. The home side won the toss, but with only 22 on the board Glenn Turner, Phil Neale and Ted Hemsley had all been dismissed. Alan Ormrod's 86 steadied the ship, but it was young wicket-keeper David Humphries whose maiden century ensured that Worcester made full use of their 100 overs. Their 304 for seven was soon looking more than competitive after they had disposed of Warwickshire for 216, Amiss top-scoring with 53. An unbeaten 80 from Neale then set up a challenging declaration, but Warwickshire, set 296 for victory in four and three quarter hours, failed to take advantage of a splendid opening partnership of 161 between Amiss and David Smith, the match ending as a draw with six wickets down.

From Worcester Tommy and Budd travelled to Oxford, where Glamorgan were the visitors. Though the Welsh county were far from full strength, it was still ritual slaughter of the undergraduates, Glamorgan's 234-run victory owing much to their overseas star Peter Swart, who scored a century and then took six wickets in the match.

A county of whom Tommy would see a great deal on his first-class travels was Gloucestershire, and his schedule now gave him seven days cricket at their Wagon Works Ground. So named because it had been created for employees of the once world-renowned Gloucester Railway Carriage and Wagon Company, it typified the outgrounds that were once so popular, staging over 150 county matches before care of the square fell into the hands of the Council and first-class cricket ended in 1992.

For matches against Essex and Derbyshire Tommy was partnered by Alan Whitehead. After a season on the minor counties, Whitehead had won a place on the first-class list in 1970. He would eventually stand in more than 600 first-class games and reach the Test panel. To Tommy he was always an excellent umpire, but one with a reputation for brooking no nonsense, though Tommy believes this led to his downfall. 'That's why he got turfed off the Test panel because he had a set to with none other than Botham. That's what the rumour was.'

Tommy saw the best of Whitehead many years later. They were standing together at Headingley in a first round match of the NatWest Trophy when a young Yorkshire bowler was having trouble in getting rid of Northumberland captain and opening bat, Graeme Morris. 'He was a handful, bellowing and shouting, demanding to know why I hadn't given him out. I'd had enough. Alan Whitehead came over from square leg and he stood in front of him and he gave him the biggest dressing down I've ever heard in my life. He said, "How long do you think you'll be suspended for? You will be suspended. We will report you. Now get on with the game and you might save yourself." He never spoke again!'

In a summer when early protective headgear often captured the headlines, a picture later in the season showed David Constant standing with a helmet bouncing on his backside after Ian Botham had decided to remove it in a Test match. 'Nobody knew what to do with them,' says Tommy. Now Gloucestershire's match against Essex provided the first instance of one of the home county's batsmen, opener Alan Tait, taking the protection that would soon become a universal feature of cricket. His attire was later to capture the attention of John Woodcock reporting for The Times, who found it 'marginally less offensive to the eye than the Amiss model though it still made him look like something out of the zoo.'

There was a rather sedate first session, but from 70 for three the fireworks began as Mike Procter, batting for just two hours and three-quarters, hit an undefeated 203 in a total of 350 for six. Procter's innings, Wisden reported, was 'the best seen on the ground since Hammond.' Essex replied with 305 for three with four batsmen passing 50, after which, with the pitch now responding to spin, Gloucestershire found batting harder in their second knock. Only when they had reached 267 for six by lunch on the third day did Procter declare. To those on the ground it seemed a cautious closure: Essex had been left only two sessions to make 313. They made steady progress, Graham Gooch scoring 50, but Procter allowed spinners David Graveney and John Childs to operate in tandem, clearly hoping to tempt the batsmen. It still looked odds on a draw until the Dominican Norbert

Phillip came in at 120 for four. Essex's replacement for Keith Boyce as their overseas player, Phillip had registered his highest score six years earlier when he had been run out for 99 in a Shell Shield match in Guyana. John Woodcock saw him as having 'the same build, the same feline movements, the same full swing of the bat, the same violent impulses as Boyce.' He now hammered his way to his only first-class hundred. Having to contend with none of the batting innovations that have come with the twenty-over game, Gloucestershire still appeared to have the match under control. To score 47 from the last four overs was surely beyond Essex. With seven wickets down, Procter continued his strategy of temptation. There were more sixes from Phillip in the next two overs as Childs went for 14 and Graveney for 17. It was time to resort to pace but, when Brian Brain was hit for 12, the final over began with just four runs required. Procter returned to the attack himself, removing Phillip caught and bowled, but it was too late. An Essex victory came with two balls to spare, taking them to fourth in the table.

This completed a double triumph for Essex, who had also had the better of the John Player encounter between the two sides on the Sunday of the festival. While Essex continued their march up the table, Gloucestershire were left licking their wounds. Still in search of a first win in any competition, they now entertained Derbyshire. With their opponents deprived of their England bowlers Mike Hendrick and Geoff Miller, Gloucestershire's 100 overs took them to 373 for six. Procter was again in imperious form with 122, but it was Zaheer Abbas, hitting his fourth century of the season, who particularly took Tommy's eye. For Tommy the easy style of Zaheer makes him the finest batsman he has ever had the pleasure of watching at close quarters. 'He always seemed to get big scores when I was umpiring. To me he was a batsman who had all the time in the world to play his shots. And he was a gentleman – there's no other word for it. You'd never see him argue. If he was given out, off he went.'

Rain restricted play next day to just under two hours, but it was time enough for the uncovered pitch to play its part as Derbyshire were dismissed for 95 with the left-arm spin of Childs bringing him five for 24, a career best. It was to be a short-lived best. On the final day, with the pitch now drying out, he took six more wickets to end with match figures of eleven for 68 as Derbyshire went down by an innings and 139 runs.

Tommy's next landmark was standing for the first time at Lord's, where Middlesex were to play Nottinghamshire. He was partnered by Jack van Geloven, with whom he had stood at Northampton the previous year. Now in his second season on the panel, van Geloven was to be one of those whose hopes of a long-term career in umpiring ended after just a few seasons. 'I wouldn't say he had a hundred per cent knowledge of the Laws,' Tommy says. 'And he liked a drink like most of them, but he did go overboard.' As a player van Geloven had joined Leicestershire from his native Yorkshire in 1956, won his cap in 1959 and gone on to perform the double in 1962 before being released in 1965. Before his fiftieth birthday he had been discarded from the umpires list. It was the second time cricket had dealt unkindly with him. 'He was always moaning that he'd never been given a benefit,' Tommy remembers.

The thrill of standing at cricket's headquarters was marred on the last day for Tommy, when he became embroiled in a situation no umpire enjoys – making decisions when there are issues with the weather or light. 'Lord's umpires don't see the light' thundered the headline to John Thicknesse's report from an early edition of the Evening Standard. Middlesex had made all the running in the match. After dismissing Notts for only 137, they had reached 371, with 102 from Clive Radley. Requiring 234 to avoid an innings defeat, Notts had only a draw to play for on the final day, when the suitability of the light made the resumption a matter of concern for the umpires.

'We were stood on the balcony looking at the dark clouds passing over the ground. A spectator started to talk to us about weather and light conditions, when along comes Mike Brearley, the Middlesex captain, who said, "Improving, don't you think? What if I bowl Edmonds and Emburey? Would you start then?" So off we went to talk to Notts. Jackie van did the talking. Randall was sat there. He said, "If you bowl the spinners, I'll bat." Out we go. Brearley sets his field – four slips, two gullies. Derek Randall walks past me. "What's going on? He's not bowling!" The penny drops and I look behind me. Twenty-five yards away in the gloom stands Wayne Daniel, ready to bowl. Randall had a bit of a confrontation with Brearley before taking his guard. "I am not facing him in this light!" Brearley says, "The light's better. Get on with it." I looked over at my colleague at square leg, who comes across. We took off the bails and walked off with the batsmen. Middlesex trudged off behind us. We walked up the steps in deathly silence, walked through the Long Room and you could have heard a pin drop.'

Only later did Tommy realise that the spectator on the balcony with whom they had been chatting had been John Thicknesse, but the reporter had not been party to the conditions on which the umpires had agreed to resume play. 'So that's a warning: never talk to strangers. They may be the press and they'll print what they want and don't always get things right.' There was further criticism of a later decision to come off while the spinners were bowling, Dicky Rutnagur in The Daily Telegraph describing the 40-minute delay as 'quite unnecessary', while Norman de Mesquita in The Times also thought there were 'unaccountable stoppages for bad light.' He expanded: 'The first came before play had even started and the second, 25 minutes after lunch, when the light looked no different from that at the start of the afternoon.' However, Rutnagur went on to suggest that the interruption may have disturbed the batsmen's concentration, and the Middlesex spinners finished the match off with time to spare.

With the passage of time, Tommy feels Mike Brearley was 'trying it on.' 'I don't blame him. He was doing the best for his team, but we called his bluff.' Tommy was to see Brearley again the following week. The match he and van Geloven were umpiring at Chesterfield was washed out for the day and they decided to drive up to Headingley to watch the Test match against Pakistan. Their TCCB passes gained the two umpires admission to the ground. There was no play when they arrived and they accepted the offer of Dickie Bird, who was officiating with Ken Palmer, to join them in their umpires' room. On the steps to the pavilion they met the two captains, Brearley and Wasim Bari, returning from having looked at the pitch. 'Brearley looked at me coming down the steps and he just said, "No hard feelings about the game at Lord's. Don't worry about your marks."' Brearley's closing comment, Tommy knew, was a reference to press reports suggesting that the umpires would have been marked down after all the comings and goings at Lord's.

The Middlesex-Notts match had paused on the Sunday to enable the same two teams to play their JPL game. Tommy recalls that, for the one-day game, the groundsman had prepared a pitch on the edge of the square. A regulation was in force that no boundary should be less than 50 yards from the middle of the pitch. To Tommy the cut strip looked too close on the Tavern side. 'I said to Jackie, "There's no way that is 50 yards." Jackie said, "We're at Lord's. You don't question it."' This was not good enough for Tommy, who returned to the pavilion and rang the groundsman. Not best pleased but wishing to keep Tommy happy, head groundsman Jim Fairbrother came round with this own tape measure. Tommy's blushes were not spared – the crucial distance proved to be 50 yards and eight inches. The short boundary was soon being peppered by Graham Barlow as Middlesex rattled up 215 for seven. Tight bowling from Daniel and Mike Selvey built up pressure, forcing the later Notts batsmen to take risks and Keith Tomlins, an occasional bowler without a previous wicket in senior cricket, cashed in with four cheap victims as the innings closed on 154 for five.

First-class umpires, 1978

*Standing (from left): Sathyaji Rao, David Evans, Barrie Meyer, Ray Julian, David Constant, Don Oslear, David Halfyard,
Tommy, Cec Pepper, Roddy Wilson, Jack van Geloven, Bill Alley, Peter Wight, Ken Palmer, Alan Whitehead
Seated: Ron Aspinall, Sam Cook, Lloyd Budd, Jack Crapp, Dickie Bird, Tom Spencer,
Eddie Phillipson, Dusty Rhodes, Arthur Jepson, John Langridge*

Amid the discord and problems of his first appearance at cricket's headquarters Tommy carries happy memories of having umpired Wayne Daniel for the first time. Another bowler of exceptional speed, he is linked with Willis in Tommy's mind. 'Another gentleman, no bother at all. Not a big appealer, not shouting in your face. He appealed. "Not out." He didn't say, "Was it going down?" or anything. He just carried on with the game.'

Vacating Lord's for the Varsity Match, Tommy crossed the Thames to The Oval and Surrey's match with Kent, where he was to witness a world-class bowler in helpful conditions. On the first day, Chris Tavaré top-scored with 64 as Kent, already leaders in a championship they were destined to win, compiled 272 for eight. Surrey then lost both their openers before the close, wicket-keeper Jack Richards and pace bowler Ray Baker standing firm as night-watchmen. The pair remained together while nine runs were added in the two overs bowled on the second day and their partnership continued into the final day, when Surrey's first aim was to avoid the follow-on – from 30 for two they needed to reach 123. All out for 95, they fell well short as Derek Underwood and Graham Johnson took four wickets each. Thereafter it was the Underwood show. Bowling from Tommy's end, the England left-armer made full use of the drying conditions to take nine for 32. The third nine-wicket haul of his career, it cost him just four runs more than when he had dismissed Sussex at Hastings 14 years earlier.

Tommy looks back on a day when covering was restricted to only four feet from the popping crease and 18 wickets fell for 149 runs. He had been in the perfect spot to watch Underwood exploit the turning pitch, all his wickets falling to catches. 'What a marvellous bowler! He had a complete circle round the bat and every ball he put it there, right on the spot for the bat pad. How they'd appeal today! It was bad enough then. But they appealed – out or not out – they never said a word. Now today it would be "Come on, umpire!"'

Tommy had stood with Cec Pepper at The Oval. Widely cited as the best Australian never to have won a Test cap, Pepper was one whose playing career was just beginning when war broke out. After a highly successful time as a professional in league cricket, he became a first-class umpire in 1964. Of a man whose fruity language had been a feature of many a dressing room, his Wisden obituarist wrote that 'he could not imagine any match involving Pepper pursuing a peaceful course, but there was usually more humour than anger.' Tommy regarded him as a good sound umpire, but one with a chip on his shoulder. 'Cec was obsessed with the fact that he couldn't get on the Test panel, when Bill Alley had made it.' Tommy remembers that supplying umpires' coats was just one of his Pepper's business side-lines. 'He came about 25 minutes before the start at The Oval, and he reckoned he'd been selling ladies' underwear at Crystal Palace out of the boot of his car.' After standing with Tommy, there were just five more championship matches for Pepper. Tommy recalls that he vented his wrath in press articles over the discrimination he had suffered in his umpiring career. It was not until 1978 that he was entrusted with a semi-final in the Gillette Cup, just days before he was off the list for good. Had he held his tongue, he might have broken through and been given a Lord's final, Tommy was led to understand.

From The Oval Tommy travelled north to meet up again with Jack van Geloven at Chesterfield. After a fair start it hadn't been the best of summers for the weather – records suggest it was one of the worst – and now, at the beginning of July, play in the championship match between Derbyshire and Sussex was ruled out early enough to allow the two umpires to escape the Queen's Park pavilion and make their trip up the motorway to Leeds and the Test match – not that there was much play for them at Headingley. The third day at Chesterfield saw the captains making an effort to set up a bonus points contest, but even this was frustrated by the returning rain. It had been the same story on the Sunday, when Glamorgan had come across from Leicester. Conditions would not have been deemed suitable for a first-class match, but the JPL was seen as family entertainment for a Sunday afternoon. And it was entertainment with a difference – the television cameras were there. 'That added to the pressure to get a game on,' says Tommy. 'They wanted to put a game on regardless of conditions.' The wish to give spectators something to watch brought a ten-over thrash. Glamorgan won the toss and decided to field. Derbyshire's batsmen, led by Eddie Barlow, then managed 62 for four from their 60 balls, a paltry total by today's standards, but when their opponents could manage no better than 44 for four, it was enough for one headline to dub them 'Dashing Derbyshire'.

The rain was still in command as Tommy made his way to Wellington in Shropshire, where he was to umpire the home county's Gillette Cup match against Surrey. There was no play on the scheduled Wednesday, so he and Dusty Rhodes could only drown their sorrows in the pavilion. The next day, there were doubts about whether the game could start on time, but prompted by a miserable forecast for the Friday, the two captains decided to delay the contest no further. Former Worcestershire player Doug Slade captained Shropshire and, on winning the toss, chose to bat on a heavily sanded pitch, opening the innings himself with Steve Johnson. The pair made slow progress. On what was proving a lifeless surface the first ten overs brought just ten runs. 'Shropshire's best attacking spell,' the local paper was able to report, 'came in the twelfth over – Knight's second – when they scored three runs.' The openers added 64, but it should never have reached this point. Johnson, who had already been dropped off a skier by Intikhab Alam, was given not out after Tommy had heard 'the most blatant of nicks' but his colleague had not done so. Rhodes had started his umpiring career in 1958 and had stood in eight Test matches, but his faculties were clearly on the wane. 'He didn't know what day it was!' Tommy reflects. The next summer Rhodes would be unable to complete his allocation of matches. Shropshire's second wicket fell at 90, but by that time they were into the 44th of their 60 overs. They scraped their way to 148 for nine, after which John Edrich made sure of a six-wicket victory, batting through for an undefeated 72 as his team-mates found the going less easy.

It was to be the last Tommy would ever see of Dusty Rhodes, who died five years later, but in the Shropshire side that day was a 26 year-old who would rise to the first-class umpires list. Steve Gale played over a hundred matches for Shropshire. Taking up umpiring when he retired, he joined the MCCA panel just before he was too old to do so. Tommy had alerted him to the age limit and he was again instrumental in persuading him to apply for the first-class list. Admitted in 2010, he has proved to be one of the distinguished few able to hold his own at the top without first-class playing credentials.

Tommy's next assignment brought him the return match between Yorkshire and Warwickshire, this time at Bradford with a switch to Headingley for the Sunday League game. These were to be the only two matches in which he stood with Ron Aspinall. Himself a Yorkshireman, now entrusted with officiating his own county, Aspinall was soon drawn into the action by Geoff Boycott, Yorkshire's captain. Tommy was certainly impressed by his fellow umpire. 'He gave Boycott out. "You're not happy. Get out," he said. Because Boycott had come moaning about us starting when it was too wet.' With Boycott out for 17 and no other batsman passing 21, John Hampshire's 132 was an innings of massive importance, and Yorkshire's 227 looked a healthier score once they had dismissed Warwickshire for 85. Dennis Amiss usually made runs when Tommy was around and he now made 46 of this miserable total, as Chris Old took six for 34. With half-centuries from Boycott and Richard Lumb, there was a declaration at 185 for three, leaving Warwickshire just over a full day to score 327. From an overnight score of 18 without loss, they made a better fist of their second effort. Neal Abberley top-scored with 81 and there were forties from Amiss and Alvin Kallicharran. At one stage well placed, Warwickshire entered the last 20 overs requiring 86 with four wickets remaining. The loss of another wicket prompted them to call off the chase, but when Old began the seventeenth over, Yorkshire still needed two wickets. Five balls later a dramatic victory had been won, David Bairstow clinging onto two catches behind the wicket.

This was a second victory for the Tykes, coming hot on the heels of success in their Sunday match, in which Bairstow had again been the hero, this time with the bat. A painstaking 56 from Lumb had threatened to derail Yorkshire's attempt to reach a modest target of 161, but Bairstow not only played his shots but put a squib up his partner to get his side home with five wickets to spare. After some years in the doldrums Yorkshire were now handily placed in both championship and JPL tables.

For all the pleasure Tommy had been getting from watching some of the world's leading cricketers at close quarters, it had been a grinding schedule with poor weather stretching back for weeks. 'I stood 29 days on the trot at one stage and Barbara told my two daughters to watch the TV so they didn't forget what I looked like!' The family had had three opportunities to see Tommy in action in a JPL match. Apart from the near farce at Chesterfield, the cameras had been on him at the Wagon Works and also when he had stood with Ron Aspinall at Leeds. There was now a short break before he was back at Bradford, this time with Don Oslear, to take charge of Yorkshire's second round match in the Gillette Cup against Nottinghamshire.

Once again rain intervened, giving Oslear plenty of time to test Tommy out on some of the more esoteric aspects of the Laws. In the time available on the first day Notts made 225 for seven, with 71 from Clive Rice, to which Yorkshire had replied with 34 without loss in 14 overs. Next day, despite a hold-up while the umpires and all the fielders searched the pitch for his contact lens, Boycott proceeded to 63. All had looked well for his side at 140 for one, but wickets then began to tumble, and at 169 for five it was a different story. Runs from Bairstow and Phil Carrick eased the tension, but both were run out in the 54th over. Graham Stevenson was caught off Rice, who then struck Howard Cooper in front with a full toss to make it 221 for nine. Five runs were still needed. A no ball and a leg bye edged Yorkshire closer. As the final over began – South African Kenny Watson to Steve Oldham – Yorkshire required three. There were two dot balls then a scythe through the covers, the ball just defying the efforts of Derek Randall and Paul Todd to stop it. The batsmen hared up and down and Yorkshire were home by one wicket.

Chapter Seven

A week never to forget – standing with Dickie Bird

The next few days were to become some of the most memorable of Tommy's season on the first-class circuit. He was to be at Trent Bridge with Dickie Bird. 'A week never to forget!' he calls it. Tommy generally travelled by train to his appointments, leaving the van for Barbara and aware that, if he took it, they would need to hire another to deliver the newspapers and for other shop business. 'I arrived late at Nottingham, something like nine o'clock at night as I had to change trains a couple of times. Dickie was sat up to the window waiting for my taxi to arrive. "Come on in!"' So began Tommy's week of partnering a legend, a man who has become perhaps the best-known umpire in the world. 'If the weather was good, he was great to stand with. He was a good decision-maker. The West Indies thought he was wonderful. Michael Holding thought he was the greatest thing since sliced bread. But he was shocking with ground, weather and light. No use to anybody. He hadn't the players' confidence; he hadn't his colleague's confidence. In lots of ways he was a lovely man, but if it rained, he was a nightmare.'

For the opening day in the first of the two championship matches in which they were to stand together, the summer conformed to its miserable pattern. Play got under way only after a delayed start, with Middlesex reaching 160 for three in the 175 minutes available. 'How delayed the start should have been can only be a matter of opinion,' wrote The Daily Telegraph's John Mason. Readers were not told what Mason's own view was, but there had been no shortage of fussing about before the decision to start was made. One man who always had a vested interest in the umpires' deliberations at Trent Bridge was Notts chief executive, Philip Carling, who was anxious to let the public know what was going on even if he couldn't promise them a start. 'I can still see him coming on the pitch that day,' says Tommy. '"Oh look who's coming!" said Dickie. "I don't get on with him. I'm not going to talk to him." And Dickie swerved round him and kept walking. "What's happening?" I said, "We're going to inspect this pitch, Mr Carling." "Thank you, Tom. That man does not like me and I do not like him!"'

There followed three days of decent, even quite good, weather. Tommy was hoping it could stay that way. When unruffled by worries about the weather or light, Bird could be good company. Though not a big drinker – he liked a gin and tonic after the game – he ate well. Each evening they went out for his favourite meal – fish and chips. 'He used to eat two lots. "Fish and chips and peas, and I'll have 'em again while you're finishing yours!"' Tommy remembers Bird, a man of changeable mood, reflecting dolefully as they chatted. 'Dickie said, "This game's killing me. Look what it's done to my pals – Syd Buller, Arthur Fagg dead. Jack Crapp, Dusty Rhodes, Ces Pepper and now Barrie Meyer all ill. It'll be me next!"' Thirty-six years later Harold Bird was alive and well as president of Yorkshire County Cricket Club. On another evening, with his companion in more jocular vein, the two umpires walked round Trent Bridge and ended up by the Nottingham Forest football ground, which was being refurbished over the summer. 'Nobody was around so Dickie said, "Let's go in." Removing a loose board in the fencing and ignoring the sign about guard dogs on patrol, we walked out onto the field. Dickie's standing on the centre spot, imagining he's umpiring a World Cup cricket match with the stands full of people.'

The fish and chips pattern was interrupted on the Sunday night, when Tommy had arranged for Barbara to come over to Nottingham to join them. The prospect of female company sent Bird into a spin. He had no suit with him, so he drove back to Barnsley to get one. Conscious that his name was emblazoned across the sides of his car, Bird was concerned that his presence might be spotted in the pub car park. 'Will Barbara drive?' he enquired of Tommy. They set off in the van with Barbara behind the wheel and Bird, in his best suit, tucked into the back in one of the seats Tommy had had fitted. 'Will she have a drink?' Bird asked on arrival, startling Tommy by returning to the table with three lagers in pint glasses with handles. 'She's driving,' Tommy protested. 'Don't worry about that. She'll be OK.' It was a merry evening, but the plan to preserve anonymity was soon shown to be hopelessly flawed. 'People kept recognizing Dickie and coming up with a pen – "Will you sign this?"'

With the sun shining on the second day, Mike Selvey, captaining the county in the absence of Mike Brearley on Test duty, recognised the need to make up for lost time and closed the Middlesex innings once a third batting point was in the bag at 250 for seven. Notts replied with 181, a total that would have been woefully inadequate had it not been for 78 from Mike Harris and 60 from skipper Mike Smedley. By the close Middlesex were 21 for one. Next day, Selvey timed his declaration to a nicety, challenging Notts to make 251 at about four an over. Surprisingly, it was not John Emburey, who took three wickets, but Norman Featherstone, bowling off spin, who now did the main damage with what was to remain a career-best five for 32 before Wayne Daniel returned to grab the last wicket with eight minutes to spare, sealing a Middlesex victory by 111 runs.

The weather held for the Saturday, the first day of the Kent match. Kevin Jarvis, with five for 74, led the way in restricting Notts to 216, to which Kent had replied with 61 without loss by the close. From this point on there was no let up with the weather. Not a ball could be bowled in the Sunday League match, allowing Bird the time to return to Barnsley for his suit. On Monday it was reported that 'umpires Bird and Wilson spent half an hour in the middle coming to a decision,' after which play was restricted to 75 minutes before lunch with another 25 after the break before the weather closed in once more. In the time allowed Kent progressed to 143 for six, with Kenny Watson making the most of a damp pitch to take four of the wickets.

Speculation over whether Kent captain Alan Ealham should declare and try to force a win or settle for batting points was looking academic next morning. 'It's clapping down. We're staying right opposite the ground in this bed and breakfast which Dickie had booked. We sat there and he couldn't eat his breakfast. He was so worried about the weather that he shot his egg and fried bread across the floor. It was twenty past eight. I said, "There's no chance. We'll not play before lunch." "I'm going over there. You can follow." So apparently he got to the ground and talked to the groundsman. By the time I got there it had stopped.'

The umpires were now into frequent inspections with the two captains sometimes accompanying them and with Bird and Carling doing their best to avoid each other. Meanwhile, as on the previous day, the press were keen to know what was going on and when play was likely to resume. Who better to ask than the umpires? 'We were in a tiny room, a long, narrow room, a bit like a broom cupboard. It had a window, but it wasn't looking out at the pitch. And people kept knocking at this door. "Go and look who it is. Don't let 'em in!" Or it was: "Oh, he's a reporter – don't let him in. Keep him out. Keep him out!"'

Meanwhile the ground staff were doing all they could to get play started. 'The groundsman said to us, "Take an early lunch. I can get you on here shortly afterwards."' This didn't satisfy Bird. '"We can't go on there – there's no way we'll play on there." Anyway up come the two captains, Mike Smedley and Alan Ealham. They'd come to some agreement. "We've worked it out if we can get on, we can both make some bonus points."' The captains made it clear that they would absolve the umpires from responsibility in their reports if they allowed the game to re-start. 'I thought that's good – we can't go wrong.' But it wasn't good enough for Dickie. 'We're not playing....' 'Well we must have gone out every half hour. Every time it was no – and he brought up water with his shoes. He was good at bringing water up. I don't know if he paddles in it, but he can bring it up anywhere.'

It was well into the afternoon before the match finally resumed. Richard Streeton in The Times reported five inspections by the umpires, but generously acknowledged that 'this should not be construed as criticism of Messrs Bird and Wilson.' Tommy for his part admits that the pitch 'wasn't brilliant', but he was delighted that they had at last got the game moving. Up came Kevin Cooper to bowl the first ball – and Tommy remains convinced that the ensuing scenario was a carefully set up prank. 'As he delivers the ball, he slides along the side of the pitch. Dickie was at square leg with a crumpled look on his face. Well he comes flying in. "This is what I said would happen." There are almost tears coming out of his eyes. "This is what I said. Nobody listens to me." The players were laughing at him and the bowler had a big smile on his face – he hadn't hurt himself. But that's the sort of thing that drove me daft with Dickie.' When the laughter had died down, the game resumed until Kent declared at 201 for nine. Thanks to 20 from Derek Underwood, with Jarvis propping up an end, they earned one more batting point and Notts secured two more for bowling. The sides departed with six points each – it could have been worse.

The mention of Mike Smedley prompts Tommy to recall an incident from the Middlesex match. 'I gave him out caught off the thumb and he didn't look happy. At lunchtime up he comes and sits beside me and Dickie sits the other side. He said, "I wasn't happy about that decision." Dickie says, "Are you saying you didn't hit it?" He said, "I'm not saying anything to you. I'm not saying I didn't hit it. Will you let me finish? I'm not talking to you – I'm talking to Tommy." And he said, "I don't think you could tell that it came off my glove. I think you were guessing." Dickie said, "I've never heard owt so silly in all my life. You're given out. You're admitting you hit it, so what are you grumbling about?" So Dickie fell out with him, not me. He fell out with him on my behalf.'

After his week at Trent Bridge Tommy was scheduled for a break, but it was not to work out as planned. And the man behind the disruption to his life was once again Dickie Bird. Wednesday, 2nd August was the date set aside for the quarter-finals of the Gillette Cup. The match at Old Trafford between Lancashire and Middlesex had been allotted to Bird and Peter Wight, a West Indian who had come to England to play in the Lancashire League later enjoying 13 successful years as a batsman with Somerset. Given the prevailing weather, it was as well that three days had been allowed for what was supposedly a one-day contest. The first day enabled Lancashire to make 279 for six with 131 from Andrew Kennedy, after which there was a single over of the Middlesex reply before the light was deemed unsuitable and play was abandoned for the day.

Here was poor Dickie Bird once more embroiled in a weather and light dispute, and Tommy learnt later how the situation escalated. 'As the umpires came off, they stopped at the bottom of the steps up to the pavilion. In those days there were a lot of people drinking and somebody threw a full pint of lager at Bird. "You're a disgrace. We've paid to come and watch cricket and you've brought them off again." Dickie then stumbled and fell on the steps, hobbled up the rest of the steps and refused to go out again.' Cedric Rhoades, Lancashire chairman, took the matter in hand and the culprit was removed from the ground and had his membership rescinded.

The following morning Tommy received a telephone call: 'Dickie's not able to take the field. Can you get to Old Trafford as soon as possible?' Tommy knew that the journey would take him the best part of an hour and a half. He had difficulty gaining admission to the ground, the gatemen protesting that both umpires had already arrived. Eventually Tommy was let in, soon finding that play had not resumed because of the light. He sped up to the umpires' room. 'Dickie was sat there in the corner, and when he's excited he twirls his hair – I've seen him do it many times. He's twirling his hair round and round with his head down. "Brilliant, brilliant – you've come." I said, "Yes, but I've not packed a tie." "Well you'll have to have a tie here." He took his tie off and gave it to me. "I'm going to Wakefield Hospital now – I'll not be umpiring on Saturday. I'm not coming here again – they're a disgrace."'

Seeing Peter Wight out on the field sitting on the covers, Tommy left Bird to his ranting and set off to join him. As he made his way out, he bumped into Frank Hayes, Lancashire's captain. 'Thank God for that,' he said, 'we've got somebody here with a modicum of sense. The sooner that chap goes home the happier I'll be. He's a bloody idiot.' Meanwhile there had been some merriment in the Lancashire dressing room, where it was known that Bird had been complaining after being hit on the leg in the field. He had gone to see the Lancashire physio, but before the incident with the beer he had started saying he wouldn't be able to carry on. So when the players saw who his replacement was, they saw the irony. 'What's Dickie been moaning about?' Jack Simmons remembers them all saying. 'He's only been bruised and he's been replaced by a man with one leg!'

Tommy went out onto the field. 'They're all shouting, "Tommy'll get some play, I'm telling you!" I get to the centre and the clouds above parted. It's fit for play! We told them to shift the covers – we're playing. Talk about being clapped off!' Tommy's heroic status was short-lived. Two spells of play brought only eight overs, enough time for him to register just how close to the umpire Colin Croft came when at full steam. Middlesex progressed to 24 for one. 'We had to come off for bad light – this time we got booed off!'

A third day was needed. There were half-centuries for Clive Radley and Mike Gatting, but Lancashire still had the upper hand. At 224 for nine it seemed all over, but John Emburey and Wayne Daniel had other ideas. They had added 34 and were in the 57th over with 22 still needed when David Hughes shouted for lbw against Daniel and Tommy's finger went up. 'The place erupted. It was in the days when crowds used to go onto the field. There were people grabbing wickets. I remember my hat – one of those flat caps like Dickie wore – that was lost.'

As they came off Peter Wight told Tommy that the Man of the Match adjudicator had not been able to attend for the third day's play, so the umpires had to nominate their man. The choice was an easy one – Andrew Kennedy. That evening, towards midnight, Tommy received a telephone call. It was Dickie Bird. 'He said, "I don't want to go back to Old Trafford, not while they're in that mood. By the way, did you pick the Man of the Match?" I said, "Yes." "Did you get paid for it?" I said, "No." "Well I'll get the cheque and I'll write you a new one."' Not long after, the promised cheque arrived from Dickie Bird. At £50, a half share of the fee intended for the original celebrity adjudicator, it was the same as the TCCB paid umpires for a three-day match.

A few years after they had stood together, Tommy travelled to Worcester with a friend to watch a match against Lancashire. Knowing that Bird would be umpiring with John Hampshire, Tommy let him know that they would be coming. Tickets awaited them at the gate: 'Guests of Harold Bird.' Later in the day bad light took the players off, so Tommy and his friend went to the umpires' room to thank for the tickets. 'I knocked on the door. Dickie comes to the door and he got hold of me, grabbed me by the shirt and pulled me into the room. "Look who's here, John! He'll know what to do! What would you do in conditions like this?" I said, "I'm glad it's not my decision!" And John Hampshire is sat with a grin on his face as much as to say – how did you put up with this?'

This was England's premier umpire, a man who had already stood in half his eventual total of 66 Tests, but one even the public had begun to associate with doom and gloom if clouds were on the horizon. 'Yes,' Tommy reflects, 'When the weather broke, he didn't know what to do. He used to go round picking people's brains. "What do you think about the weather?" "What do you think?" But in so many ways he was a lovely man.'

Chapter Eight

The end of the first-class dream

Tommy was learning that life on the first-class panel wasn't always a bed of roses. He well remembers the day when he and Arthur Jepson were together at Bradford for a JPL match against Sussex. The visitors had made 200 for eight in their 40 overs when rain intervened. In the days long before the Duckworth Lewis method had been invented, the side batting second had only to beat their opponents' run rate to win the match. With time for no more than the ten overs that would constitute a match, Sussex were required to make only 51, a modest target given that there would be no penalty for losing wickets.

With Javed Miandad and Imran Khan sent in to open, it looked plain sailing. And so it proved. After 8.2 overs the target had been reached, at which point David Bairstow, the Yorkshire keeper, helpfully pulled up the stumps. 'But Arthur Jepson shouts out, "Hang on, hang on. You've not played ten overs – it's no result."' There were two experienced scorers, Yorkshire's Ted Lester and Geoffrey Saulez, who had kept the book in Tests. Certain that the match was over, they left their box, refusing to record the final ten balls that Jepson insisted should be bowled. The extra deliveries were played around the field, a few more runs were taken and the Sussex victory was confirmed.

But what had the umpires been up to? 'I was wrong,' Tommy admits,' but so was Arthur and I looked on him as the senior umpire. The scorers went berserk. Arthur insisted he was right. It was Sunday, of course, but he managed to get hold of someone at Lord's. "We'll ring you back." Well it was ten to eight when they rang back. Arthur gets hold of the phone. He says, "Bloody hell. We're wrong." I can see his face!' There had been some ambiguity in the regulations that was ironed out for the next season, but the press had a field day. 'Thank God John Hampshire was captain and not Boycott,' Tommy reflects, 'or all hell would have been let loose.' To Tommy, Jepson remained a lovely man. 'A down-to-earth, engaging fellow, he was well liked by the players.' It was just as well. Such umpires are excused the odd faux pas. It is a view John Hampshire endorses after all the years. To John the abiding memory of Jepson is of a man ready to have a laugh, whilst also having been a very good umpire.

Tommy should have enjoyed more of Jepson's company on the field, but the championship match that sandwiched the farcical affair at Bradford comprised only 89 overs, during which Yorkshire reached 252 for six shortly before lunch on the third day. There was a declaration at this point, but the players were never to return to the field. Shortly after two o'clock 'a spectacular climax of thunder, lightning and torrential rain' ensured abandonment, leaving Yorkshire with three points and Sussex with two.

Tommy now returned to The Oval where Glamorgan were to be the visitors. He was to stand with one of the younger umpires on the list, Ray Julian, a former wicket-keeper for Leicestershire and one who enjoyed life on the umpiring circle. For once they did not have to contend with the weather. Fortunate to win the toss, Surrey made best possible use of a good pitch. Alan Butcher, with 176, and Roger Knight, who made 119, took the county to 403 for five in their 100 overs. Tommy remembers that among those on the ground to see Butcher's fine innings was a little lad of about six – it was young Mark, destined to upstage his one-cap father and score eight centuries for England. Glamorgan lost two early wickets, ending on 34 for two before the players broke off for the Sunday game. This was to prove a tightly fought affair with ramifications that would spill over into the championship match. Choosing to bat first, Glamorgan made 222 for three, with Alan Jones and Peter Swart enjoying an unbeaten partnership of 137. It was a target Surrey were always struggling to reach, but Intikhab Alam, promoted to number five, David Smith and Monte Lynch made up lost ground.

At 206 for six Lynch was joined at the wicket by Robin Jackman. With every run crucial, Jackman ventured too early from his crease and the bowler, left-arm seamer Alan Wilkins, broke the wicket and appealed. Such an action was widely held to be 'not cricket' and it had not happened in the championship since 1956 when another Welshman, the colourful Glamorgan captain Wilfred Wooller, had sent Essex batsman Gordon Barker on his way. Now, in the heat of battle at The Oval, there were no preliminary pleasantries, and no warning was given – Tommy gave Jackman out. 'I looked at Alan Jones and said, "Do you wish the appeal to stand?" "Yes," he said, so I said to Robin, "Sorry, Robin, you're out."' Eventually five runs were needed off the last over. Wicket-keeper Jack Richards was run out, leaving the scores level with one ball remaining, but Lynch held his nerve and took Surrey over the line.

Next day the championship game resumed, and bowling from Tommy's end was a still enraged Jackman. 'He hit Jones on the pad and he let out this huge appeal and went down on his knees in front of me like he was praying. "Give him out! Give him out!" And there was the odd f-word in it! I could see that confrontation coming.' 'He was always one of the mouthiest appealers,' fellow umpire Ray Julian comments. Glamorgan managed only 205 and followed on thanks to the efforts of the Surrey spinners Pat Pocock and Intikhab, while Jackman leaked 43 runs from nine wicketless overs. Glamorgan made a better fist of their second innings, Intikhab having to work hard for his six wickets as Rodney Ontong battled to a century for Glamorgan. Requiring 146 to win, Surrey stuttered at first. Three wickets were down for only 32, but Butcher and Graham Roope saw their side to a seven-wicket win shortly after tea, only darkening clouds threatening the success of their mission.

The season was now coming towards a close. A championship match at Bristol saw Middlesex march on with a seventh win in eight matches in their bid to retain the title they had shared with Kent in 1977. After they had bowled the home side out for 187 well before tea on the first day, Roland Butcher hit his first century in senior cricket as Middlesex reached 329 in only 80 overs. The match was rushing ahead of schedule, and when Gloucestershire could stretch their second innings to only 26.2 overs, it was completed well inside two days. Defeated by an innings and 14 runs, the Gloucestershire team were told it would be extra nets – their poor play had not earned them a day off!

Tommy had been with Peter Wight at Bristol. Wight was not one of the umpiring fraternity to be found laughing and joking with the players. Like David Constant, he preferred to keep his distance, and as with Cec Pepper, Tommy detected discontent that his long service on the first-class panel had not been better rewarded with international recognition or a Lord's final. The pair drove together in Wight's car to Leicester, where bottom-of-the-table Northants were the visitors, to be followed by Nottinghamshire. Illustrating the way umpires helped each other, Ray Julian had fixed them up with bed and breakfast about 100 yards from the ground where he had played his cricket. Tommy still retains the letter that told him Mrs Scofield would be charging four pounds a night, a handy saving on the TCCB allowance.

The first championship match ended in a tame draw, with Leicestershire comfortable winners in the Sunday game. Ray Illingworth had missed the three-day match against Northants, but he returned for the visit of Nottinghamshire. Billed as the former England captain's farewell to first-class cricket, the match started well for Leicestershire. There was a sparkling 142 from Ian Davison and a reminder of Illingworth's perennial skill as an off-spinner when he took six for 38 to give Leicestershire a commanding lead of 154. It was enough to enforce the follow-on, but a blank second day left too little time for Leicestershire to reap the reward their dominance had deserved. The match ended when the umpires offered the batsmen the light with 12 overs to go. On 46 for four Notts were only too happy come off. There had been time for Illingworth to take what was regarded as a final first-class scalp when he bowled Pasty Harris. Though they were not to know it, the pundits were well wide of the mark. Four years later, Illingworth, by then manager of Yorkshire, would return to first-class cricket for two more summers, choosing to demonstrate in the middle what he could only talk about from beyond the boundary.

For Tommy it was back to Edgbaston for one last John Player League match – and a cracker it proved to be with Gloucestershire, bottom of the table, sneaking only their third win of the season off the final ball of the match. Earlier Tommy had had to give Dennis Amiss run out for 99.' As he passed me at square leg, he said "How have I scored over 2000 runs this season with you umpiring?" I replied, "Hang on, how many times have I given you out when you were well past 50?" Dennis just smiled.'

The final championship match of Tommy's season was at Worcester, where interest centred on whether a young Ian Botham, still with his greatest years ahead, could crown a fine season by taking his hundredth first-class wicket. He came in search of six more victims. After a truncated first day he had three. Next morning, he claimed three more, the last when he dismissed opener Alan Ormrod, who had come close to carrying his bat, for a diligent 116. It had been a close run thing with Ormrod earlier missed, off the same delivery, by third slip, second slip and then keeper Trevor Gard, but it was Gard who made amends a few balls later. A match kept alive by positive declarations saw Vic Marks and Keith Jennings unable to score 18 from the final over. This came after Philip Slocombe, seen at the time as one of the brightest stars of the future, had failed by just two runs to register a second century in the match.

It was all over. Tommy's marks for the season had not reached the level he would have expected in the minor counties. Of the 24 umpires he was placed 22nd in first-class matches and, as far as he can recall, 17th or 18th in one-day games. He had been warned by colleagues that his status as a non-player would always be an obstacle. 'I got told by other umpires, "If you get well marked and do well, you really will have done well. Don't forget you've never played the game and some captains might not like that."' Some captains spoken to from that era admitted that there might always have been some subconscious mistrust of those who had not played the first-class game; but in John Hampshire's view, 'some captains who didn't know him as well as they ought to have done will have seen his infirmity and marked him down. We never had a complaint.' Sussex captain Arnold Long wrote to the TCCB on Tommy's behalf, while he received a letter from David Constant expressing his view that Tommy had not been given a fair chance to establish himself. 'I can't understand why you've come off,' the respected Test umpire said.

The belief that former players will make the best umpires is an attitude that prevails today and it is one which Paul Adams, in his role assisting ECB umpires manager Chris Kelly in assessing those striving for a place on the list, fully understands. A career schoolmaster, Paul enjoyed 11 years as a first-class reserve. He is, in Tommy's view, the best non-first-class umpire with whom he has stood. Paul had owed much in his early days to a friendship with Nigel Plews, with 11 Tests the most successful of all post-war umpires without playing credentials. 'Chris Kelly and I are both very conscious that first-class cricket is a tight-knit circle, and if you are not part of it, there's a bit of suspicion really,' Paul says. 'We take the view that, if you're an ex-player, you have got a much better chance of making it – being accepted and being able to do the job efficiently as well.'

Paul Adams (left), the best umpire Tommy stood with on the minor counties circuit, with Neil Bainton, a non-first-class cricketer now established on the first-class umpires' panel

Paul expands on the natural advantages the ex-player enjoys: 'He's familiar with their dressing room, he's familiar with their players. He feels more at home, whereas when I went to do a first-class game, everything was 100 mph, far quicker than anything I'd ever done. I'd got to learn the game all over again. It took me a while and I still maintain that, if you were to ask those umpires on our first-class list now who are not ex-professional cricketers, they still feel it's a club they haven't quite broken into, even though they've been round the block for many years.' Even his friend Nigel Plews, Paul suspects, never felt wholly within the circle.

In due course Tommy was informed that he would not be retained on the panel for the 1979 season. The decision was not wholly due to his marks, he was told, but there was a fear that he would be unable to give the years of service TCCB would expect for a first-class umpire due to his disability. Any attempt to analyse Tommy's ability as an umpire cannot escape returning to his impediment. Naturally he was disappointed to lose his place on the first-class list, but he insists there were no sour grapes. He had been given his chance and he accepts that a few years later there would have been no way an umpire with his physical impediment would have been considered. 'He would never have got on the list today,' countless people have said, though Chris Kelly, umpires manager at the ECB, is not one of them, pointing to the remarkable feats of disabled athletes in other fields. Tommy himself is more philosophical, wondering at how well he would cope with the physical tests which umpires of the 21st century must undergo. 'I can always say – been there, done that, got the tee shirt,' he still says with a broad grin.

It had seemed a curious decision by the TCCB to introduce to the panel in the same year two umpires with physical disabilities, and Tommy still wonders if the presence of Roddy Wilson had worked to his disadvantage. 'He made a big thing of it, being put off because of his disability. He got the same letter – you were dropped partially but not wholly because of the marks, but your disability we've taken into consideration. He took offence to that. I didn't. He even got Alf Morris involved.' Labour MP Alf, later Lord, Morris had always championed the rights of disabled people. In 1974 he had been made Minister for the Disabled, the first such appointment in the world. It was to no avail. 'To this day,' Tommy reflects, 'I believe that, had Roddy not been on the list with me, I might have been kept on it. But if they were putting one of us off, they had to put both off with the way they phrased the letter.'

Chapter Nine

Widening horizons in non-first-class cricket

Coming off the first-class list may have dampened Tommy's spirits for a short while, but it did nothing to reduce his passion for cricket or his wish to remain involved in umpiring at the highest level he could achieve. He was regarded as one of the minor counties' most respected umpires and as David Armstrong, soon to take over as MCCA secretary, was well aware, his value was the greater for being self-employed and able to take time off from the shop at short notice. He would increasingly find himself chosen for many of the more prestigious appointments within MCCA cricket, a reward for annual marks that rose after his time in the first-class game. He would be called on for early NatWest matches and before long unexpected requests to umpire overseas would also come his way. Off the field he would be putting even more back into the game he loved with the administration and evaluation of umpires and with the training of entrants to officiating and offering practical help to those rising up the ladder.

The 1978 season in which Tommy had been on the first-class list had been marked by the side effects of the Packer affair. The Australian media mogul Kerry Packer had failed to persuade the Australian Cricket Board that his television station, Channel Nine, was the one to which a contract for the coverage of Australian Test cricket should be given. Rebuffed by the board, he had set up his own cricketing circus, World Series Cricket, to which he had lured many of the leading cricketers from across the globe, promising them rewards far beyond those to which they could ever aspire within the established regime.

With a former England captain, the South Africa-born Tony Greig, acting surreptitiously as a key recruiting agent during the spring and summer of 1977, Packer had managed to divide the cricket world into what many would see as loyalists and mercenaries. Others were quicker to acknowledge that the restrictive practices seen throughout cricket were ensuring that those who earned their living from the game could never cash in on their commercial value as top performers in other sports were increasingly able to do, and such people could see that it was time to loosen those restrictions. As arguments raged after the first World Series season in Australia, there was much bad feeling in some county dressing rooms. Efforts were made to ban from the domestic game those who had enriched themselves through Packer. Derek Underwood and Alan Knott were two whose Test careers had seemed to be at an end, while there was an announcement in August that Dennis Amiss would not be offered a new contract by Warwickshire. This, of course, never happened, Amiss playing on until 1987 and later serving as the county's chief executive, but it was an example of a county bowing to the TCCB line, whereas others were more anxious not to lose their best players, many of whom were overseas stars.

A swift consequence of Packer's attack on the established game was an improvement in the rewards available to Test players the world over, not least in England. Eventually it would be argued that the bread and butter county professional had benefited from the greater commercial awareness of the game's marketability, but before all this the TCCB was to suffer an embarrassing loss in the High Court in an action that began as the 1978 domestic season came to a close.

The winter of 1978/79 was to be the second of Packer's World Series. He needed umpires and Tommy was a free agent. Though Tony Greig had played only once that summer when Tommy was umpiring, in the rain-ruined match at Chesterfield, Tommy got on well with him and now decided to write a personal letter. 'I kept it quiet for a while that I had written,' he admits. From Sydney Greig replied that he had read the letter with interest and that it had been forwarded to the managing director of World Series, who was responsible for hiring umpires. A further letter from Austin Robertson, a director of World Series, arrived on their headed paper. It thanked Tommy for his interest and explained that there would be changes and additions to their umpiring panel. Assuring him that his letter would be on file, Robertson added: 'I have spoken to Tony and others and they speak highly of your efforts.' Tommy heard no more and, by the following winter, there had been a rapprochement between the warring parties and World Series cricket was at an end.

When the 1979 cricket season came round, there were seven matches for Tommy in the Minor Counties Championship, but there was an unexpected bonus. Asked to help out when illness struck the first-class panel just as the Prudential World Cup was getting under way, he was only too pleased to accept the two matches offered. It meant standing at Worcester for the visit of Gloucestershire and then accompanying the away team on the short journey to the Wagon Works Ground at Gloucester, where they were to play Kent. On both occasions he was to accompany an umpire in his first season on the panel. The former Leicestershire pace bowler Terry Spencer would serve for five years without finding the satisfaction he had enjoyed as a player, while Derek Dennis, a Welshman with no first-class playing experience, was destined to join the list of those who failed to impress sufficiently and lasted just two seasons. Spencer was to prove a useful man to the minor counties umpires, facilitating their annual meeting at Grace Road, where he ran the bar.

At Worcester, five wickets for David Partridge helped Gloucestershire gain a lead of 100 as the home county were dismissed for 149. When Gloucestershire batted a second time, Partridge's 59 became the first half-century of the match. Set 285 to win, Worcestershire were quickly on the receiving end of the finest spell of bowling Tommy has ever witnessed. Mike Procter, with eight for 32, recorded his best figures in 12 years of English cricket to give his county a 165-run win. Only once, for Rhodesia against Transvaal in 1972, had he returned a better analysis. With his distinctive action bowling off the wrong foot, mainly round the wicket on that day, he amazed Tommy. Spreading out his hands to indicate the movement Procter achieved, he tries to explain. 'He pitched it that much outside off stump and it cut back. He cut it back in to take the stumps. You just didn't expect it. Marvellous bowler – and he was quick.'

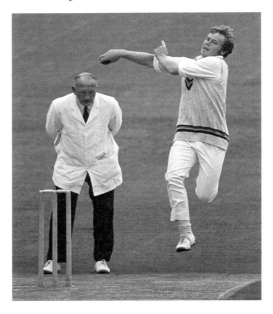

Mike Procter

It was a different story for Gloucestershire at the Wagon Works. Without Zaheer Abbas and Sadiq Mohammad, both playing for Pakistan in the World Cup, they were a weak batting side. Dismissed for 154, they had not used up their 100 overs, the balance of which accrued to Kent, for whom Charles Rowe made 102 and skipper Alan Ealham 87, as they reached 389. Early on the third day it was all over with Kent victorious by an innings and 158 runs. Derek Underwood, who had taken four wickets in the first innings, now took six for 24. Underwood had also mesmerised the Gloucestershire batsmen on the Sunday with three for 5 from his eight overs as Gloucestershire replied pitifully to Kent's 169 for eight, using 36 overs to scratch their way to 107.

Championship cricket would make no further calls on Tommy, but life was moving on apace. Apart from his on-field commitments the wider aspects of the game were also taking up much of his time. He was to continue as chairman and then president of the local Bretherton club; he remained on the executive of the Southport & District League, which he had joined in 1967 and in which Bretherton played; in his own Northern League he was now vice-chairman of its Umpires Association and soon to take over in a still-unbroken role as chairman. Tommy had also been an early recruit when the ACU sought instructors for its courses, and in 1974 he had been appointed an examiner. Tommy's courses were usually conducted over eight evenings, and he ran them in a wide range of venues in his area, qualifying around 250 umpires before passing the training duties on to others only after the ECB ACO had replaced ACU&S and introduced its Level 1a course.

Among those who attended and enjoyed the humour that characterised Tommy's classes only two or three were ladies. Tommy remembers one who went on into the league. 'I wanted her to go and umpire ladies' cricket,' he says, 'but she wouldn't. I said, "You'll go all the way to the top and umpire Test matches."' But his pupil preferred men's cricket. Meanwhile recent women's Test matches, once controlled by umpires of their own gender, have seen male officials, one first-class and one from the reserve list, taking charge. Tommy wonders if this is a healthy development. He has seen, too, just one female umpire, Lorraine Elgar, come and go on the MCCA list, standing in 14 matches across five summers. Was she a victim of male chauvinism? Maybe, but Tommy remembers her enlivening a pre-season umpires' meeting. They had all stayed overnight in a hotel. After a drink or two Tommy retired to his room. Next morning he found he had mislaid his glasses. His first enquiries failed to locate them in the bar area. 'Lorraine Elgar was sat the other side of the room. She said, "Tommy, I think you left them in my room." The whole place erupted.'

Away from cricket Tommy was leading a full life. There was always the business to look after, and in April 1969 he and Barbara had had a second daughter, Marie, ensuring that there were always plenty of family commitments. When cricket spared him on a Sunday, he might be found reading the lesson in the church where he had helped as a Sunday School teacher in his teenage years. He was regularly engaged on community issues, eventually clocking up 29 years as a local councillor. Involvement with the council had been prompted by Tommy and Barbara's concern at the speed with which traffic tore along Bretherton's South Road, close to where they were living and the road to which they have since moved. To anyone visiting the area today it seems incredible that there should ever have been no speed restriction, but Tommy was successful in getting a 40 mph limit introduced and in due course this was reduced to 30. 'Now, when the lights are flashing at school times, everybody has to slow down to 20,' he says with some satisfaction. The other big concern where Tommy and Barbara's campaigning was successful was in bringing a main sewerage system to the village. 'There were only septic tanks and bucket toilets in them days,' says Tommy, talking of a time as late as the early 1970s. He reckons it took 12 years for action to take place.

Many winter evenings were taken up enjoying snooker, the one sport where his physical handicap did not prove too much of a disadvantage to Tommy. The snooker club where he has always played is now part of the village's enlarged sporting facilities at the back of Tommy and Barbara's present home. Started in 1911 as a working men's club – for playing billiards rather than snooker initially – it offered membership from the age of 14, and this was when Tommy first joined. Many years later, when the club opened its doors to women, Barbara was the first lady member. In early married life especially, Tommy played regular team snooker in the Southport & District League. He continued doing so until 2004, when he signed off as captain of the club's third team that won the league's third division. There is an honours board with the names of a very select few club members who have managed a break of a hundred – and a half-century always eluded Tommy. 'We were only amateurs,' he stresses.

In 1982 both Tommy and Barbara took up bowls on the crown green that is close to the snooker hall. Crown green bowls is the traditional northern version of the sport, played across a convex green. Tommy's earlier bowling experience had been on flat greens, where he had been taken early in the morning by umpire Alan Whitehead, when they were together on the first-class list. It was in 1982 that the Bretherton green was restored to its original use, the area having been devoted for many years to tennis, a game for which separate provision was then made.

Changes in the format of the first-class counties' longest-standing one-day competition were soon to open up new opportunities for Tommy. In 1981 the National Westminster Bank took over sponsorship of what had hitherto been the Gillette Cup. As well as including either Scotland or Ireland, the NatWest competition initially made room for five of the minor counties, as the Gillette had done, but from 1983 the competition was opened up to provide 13 places for which the minor brethren could scrap in their own championship, while also making room for both Scotland and Ireland each year. This meant that 16 first round matches were now played, and it was well beyond the resources of the first-class panel to provide the 32 umpires needed. Thus the best minor counties officials were called up to augment the pool. For 12 years the first round of the NatWest would now be inked into Tommy's diary. There was then a five-year gap until 1999, the year in which ECB decreed that County Board sides drawn from recreational cricketers in each of the first-class counties should also be included. This move entailed two rounds of matches, soon to be played at the end of the preceding season, before the first-class counties took the field. The new arrangement brought Tommy a further nine matches, the last in 2002, his final season on the MCCA list.

In the earlier spell Tommy's colleague for these matches always came from the first-class list. It meant renewing acquaintance with Ray Julian and Alan Whitehead, standing for the first time with later entrants, some of whom he had umpired as players– Jack Birkenshaw, John Hampshire, Barry Leadbeater and David Shepherd – as well as others new to the list since 1978, Roy Palmer, Kevin Lyons and Jack Bond. With at least eight non-first-class umpires called upon, there were fears among some of the top umpires that they might be paired with someone not quite up to the job. John Hampshire, who went on to umpire 21 Tests and is now an appointed mentor for those on ECB's first-class list, speaks of 'club umpires who had passed all their exams, but we were never too sure of their decision making.' But he adds, 'With Tommy I never doubted his decision making.'

The single match in which Tommy stood with David Shepherd, not yet a Test umpire, was in 1983. They were at Wellington for Shropshire's match with Somerset, an encounter that would give Tommy his first sight at close quarters of Viv Richards. 'What a player! He would come down the track to the quicker bowlers and bang – his bat always seemed to be that wide.' In a match extended to two days because of rain, Richards top scored with 74 in a Somerset total of 246, which brought them victory by 87 runs. But the local paper showed the great man's off stump in mid-air, bowled for only 11 by fast bowler Steve Ogrizovic. Better known as a soccer goalkeeper, at that time with Shrewsbury Town but later to enjoy a long and distinguished career with Coventry City, Ogrizovic did indeed uproot Richards' stump – but Tommy had called no ball. 'Whether Richards heard the call or not, I don't know. But he was very pleased to see my arm go out.'

The early season NatWest matches also gave Tommy his first experience of standing with Barrie Meyer, the Test umpire whose serious illness had extended Tommy's workload in his year on the list. 'We got on well together. We were going to be at Headingley. I rang him up. He said, 'I'll book you in. We'll have a twin room – it'll be cheaper." I remember coming to the hotel. He said, "I've got the room worked out." And we sat and watched the World Cup.' This was 1990, when the competition was held in Italy. It was a memorable evening for the two umpires, in which they celebrated together as they watched England beat Belgium to qualify for the quarter-finals thanks to a last gasp goal from David Platt that just prevented the match going to penalties.

The early NatWest matches were widely regarded as potential banana skins by the first-class counties, especially when played on a questionable minor county surface; but there were few instances of giant-killing. Tommy's matches brought a string of particularly convincing, and sometimes embarrassingly easy, victories, his match with Meyer a typically comfortable ten-wicket win for Yorkshire against Norfolk. But among the 12 matches Tommy umpired there was one cliff-hanger, when Cheshire met Northamptonshire in 1988.

For this match, at the Chester Boughton Hall Ground, Tommy was paired with Jack Birkenshaw. Cheshire won the toss and asked Northants to bat. In difficult conditions for batting, a side whose top five all played Test cricket made slow progress. Skipper Geoff Cook opened with Wayne Larkins, but by the time the score had reached 88, Larkins, Rob Bailey, Allan Lamb and David Capel had all been dismissed, four different bowlers sharing the wickets. Cook battled on to the end for 53 not out, but his side could muster only 161, losing their last wicket with more than four overs unused. Three former Lancashire players headed the Cheshire order, Barry Wood, David Varey and Ian Cockbain. Wood made a dogged 40 before he was run out. This was a tight decision that Tommy was called on to make, and it had seemed the turning point for Northants as they continued to work their way through the Cheshire batting, but at 129 for seven it was still either side's match. At 150 for nine, with numbers ten and eleven at the crease, 11 runs needed and 25 balls left, the first-class county seemed favourites to squeeze home. But it was not to be. Andrew Fox and John O'Brien stood firm, the winning boundary coming when Fox edged the penultimate ball to the boundary. On only six previous occasions had a first-class county lost to one of the minors.

Word that an upset was on the cards had reached Granada, the local independent television station. 'I remember the vans roaring onto the ground with the cameras on top.' They were there in good time for the final rites and the celebrations. They also managed to catch Tommy's run out decision, and when he got home later that evening, Barbara was able to reassure him that he had been correct.

Chapter Ten

Eastern assignments: the Maccabiah Games and the Gulf States

July 1981 brought Tommy his first umpiring assignment overseas. When he flew out from Heathrow, he was heading for Israel where the eleventh Maccabiah Games were to be held. Every four years, in the year following the Olympic Games, Jewish people the world over gather for the games. This time teams from 34 countries were to take part, with cricket among the 28 different sports featured. Tommy's chance to go to Israel sprang from knowing two Jewish brothers who played for St Annes and whose father sometimes came to watch them. The father approached Tommy and asked him, 'How would you fancy going to Israel to do the Maccabiah Games?' When Tommy learnt what it entailed and expressed interest, the father said he would write to Neil Myeroff, the member of the British Organising Committee responsible for cricket.

A reference was required and WT 'Robbie' Robins of the ACU's North Western Region, who knew Tommy well, wrote in glowing terms, setting out his on-field credentials and also alluding to Tommy's 'very pleasant disposition'. He assured Myeroff that whatever Tommy was called upon to do, he carried out his duties 'with efficiency and good humour.' One evening a short while later, Tommy received a telephone call from Donald Carr, who explained that he too had received a letter at the TCCB asking about Tommy's suitability to officiate at the games. He said he had commended him without hesitation. Tommy was one of four umpires booked to travel, the others flying in from Australia, Zimbabwe and Ireland.

Among the countries sending large numbers of participants were the United States with 400 and Argentina and South Africa with 250 each, while the party from the host country totalled 600. The games were held at a time of isolation for South Africa, whose sportsmen were now banned from seven events because of the need to adhere to the restrictions imposed by the International Olympic Committee, but Jewish cricketers were free to take part and their team was soon to prove the strongest at the games.

Tommy arrived in stifling heat. He was housed in a comfortable hotel, but with several top FIFA officials recruited to referee the football matches, he found himself in a twin room with a German. It wasn't the ideal arrangement. 'He arrived very late on the first night. He couldn't speak a word of English and he was never off the phone, ringing home.' Language was to continue to pose problems on the field. Tommy found that Hebrew was the common language for all competitors at the games. 'I didn't know what the hell they were on about. They could have been saying anything about us!'

Playing conditions were primitive. Tommy's first match was a friendly in Beersheba, the largest city in the Nagev desert of southern Israel. In 1948 it had been no more than a tented village, but by the time of Tommy's visit it had grown to a city of 150,000. As at the other venue used for the tournament, the playing area stretched out into the desert with not a blade of grass in sight, while tents and makeshift canvas awnings acted as pavilions and shielded the few spectators the games attracted. The matches, all limited overs, were played on coconut matting stretched over wet sand that had baked in the sun. To protect the matting the umpires had to ensure that all the players were wearing boots without spikes, and a novel problem for Tommy was keeping the stumps in the ground. 'As it dried out, they'd be coming up to bowl and, never mind bails going, the wicket would topple and the two outside stumps would go different ways.'

There was also a very strange rule for wides. 'The matting was roughly eight foot wide. If the ball didn't pitch on the matting but pitched in the sand, you called "Wide". On some occasions the ball pitched in the sand, cut in and actually bowled the batsman. But it was still a wide.' The roughness of the outfield meant that the ball quickly became ragged and a regular supply of sticking plasters was needed for slip fielders whose hands were skinned when they fielded the ball. With the temperature passing 110 F, play was constantly stopping for drink breaks. 'Every half an hour a little man would run on with a muslin sack with a large lump of ice inside which he would break up with a huge rusted pick, so what you actually got was a lump of ice to suck.' Despite all the difficulties Tommy was impressed by the standard of play of some of the teams. The South Africans, who beat England in the final, he thought 'were a hell of a side.' Their generosity also left a mark: 'When they went home, they took nothing with them. They left all their bats, pads and the rest of their gear for the Israeli kids and up and coming cricketers to play with, which I thought was marvellous.' Sadly the players' kindness counted for nothing. By the third of Tommy's visits, in 1989, the ban preventing South Africa's sportsmen engaging in international cricket had stretched to the Maccabiah Games.

Each visit saw playing standards and facilities improving, and by 1989 matches were taking place in a properly appointed stadium with artificial pitches specially laid in grass outfields. The pitches were similar to the one Tommy had encountered at Preston North End's Deepdale ground in 1986 when he umpired a floodlit 30-over match between Clive Lloyd's World Eleven and West Indies. Tommy was always kept busy in Israel, umpiring on as many as eight of the ten days he was there on one trip, but he still found time to visit many of the local tourist attractions. The organisers laid on some special trips and he was also able to make free use of the bus service with his VIP games badge. So he was able to see a country with a rich history stretching back to before the time of Christ yet also bearing the scars of more modern conflict, the War of Independence in 1948 and the Six Day War in 1967.

An organised trip around Jerusalem during the 1985 games emphasised the contrasts. Along the road to the city the visitors saw the burnt-out remains of armoured trucks that had been ambushed in attempts to breach Arab blockades. Entering the city they passed through an industrial area with factories and housing erected for new immigrants in the 1950s, then saw Ammunition Hill, the site of one of the most important battles in 1967. They took in Mount Scopus, the original site of the Hebrew University with recently-built faculties on land reclaimed in 1967. There was a fleeting glimpse across the Jordan Valley to the Dead Sea; then they travelled on to the Mount of Olives and the Western Wall, where Jews have come throughout the centuries to lament the destruction of their temple and pray for its restoration.

The games in Israel also had their share of social functions. One year the cricket umpires joined referees from other sports in hosting a reception of their own. Tommy was one of those who volunteered to go round serving wine, topping up guests' glasses. 'I spotted a lovely lady and approached her with my bottle. "Say when," I said. "You're nice," she said smiling. Again I said, "Say when." "Eight o'clock?" she replied. "No, no, I mean how much?" I said. She whispered, "Twenty-five shekels." That was about £1.25. I hastily retreated.'

The memory of the incident prompts Tommy to relate another story he heard while umpiring. 'A long-suffering husband and his wife went on holiday to Jerusalem, but while they were there, the wife died. The local undertaker told the husband, "You can have her shipped home for 16,000 shekels or you can have her buried here in the Holy Land for 800 shekels." After a moment's thought, the husband said, "I think I'll have her shipped home". "Well, it's your decision" said the undertaker, "but I must say I'm surprised. Why spend 16,000 shekels on having your wife shipped back to Britain when for just 800 you could have her buried right here?" "Listen", said the husband, "many years ago, a man died here, was buried, and three days later he rose from the dead. I just can't take that risk!"'

In 1989 Barbara and Marie followed Tommy out on his trip to Israel. They stayed separately at the hotel in Tel Aviv-Jaffa where Tommy and other officials were being put up, taking advantage of an excellent bus service to see the sights of Jerusalem and Galilee while Tommy was engaged umpiring. The games all passed off peacefully until the closing ceremony when a religious sect assembled to protest against it being held at the famous Western Wall. Drowning out the prime minister's speech with shouting and screaming, they let off tear gas. Two thousand people stampeded to escape from the only open gate. Tommy was lucky to be sitting beside a man who realised the seriousness of the situation and managed to usher him to safety.

This was to be the last time Tommy went to the Maccabiah Games, but in 1992 he was invited to go to the Middle East to umpire two matches between India and Pakistan, one at Muscat in Oman, the other in Dubai. He first heard of the possible appointment on Wednesday 19th August, when he was at Blackpool umpiring a three-day second eleven match between Lancashire and Warwickshire with David Constant. It was the second day of the match when a telephone call came through for Constant, who passed on a message that there was an opportunity for an umpire who was not on the first-class list to take charge of these two matches. Scheduled for 3rd and 4th September, they would be played at a time when most first-class umpires would be engaged with championship games. However, Tommy was initially told that Barrie Meyer would be partnering him, though events that were soon to unfold contributed to the TCCB's decision not to release him.

This was a sensitive time for Anglo-Pakistani relations on the cricket field. Three days after the call had come through to Blackpool an issue that had been simmering throughout the summer came to a head, ball tampering. That Saturday England played Pakistan in a one-day international at Lord's. Chasing 205 to win, England were 145 for five when the two umpires, John Hampshire and Roy Palmer, examined the ball and changed it under Law 42. It was their belief that it had been subjected to tampering, a view endorsed by third umpire Don Oslear. For many close to the game, this was the public culmination of a dubious practice that had been going on all summer. Others would hold that such claims were without a shred of justification and merely illustrated a sour grapes attitude by English authorities when the truth was that Pakistan had more skilful bowlers whose mastery of 'reverse swing', a new concept at the time, was an art English bowlers could not match. At Lord's that day there was an orchestrated conspiracy of silence with one piece of deliberate misinformation: it was said that the ball was replaced because it had gone out of shape. The ball in question never surfaced for public examination. For Deryck Murray, the match referee, who played his part in the wall of silence, it was the end of a career in international refereeing that comprised just three ODIs. In the years ahead there would be unedifying court cases and revelations as lips that were buttoned at the time of the incident were later able to speak more freely.

Tommy needed to make swift plans if he were to accept the invitation. An immediate problem was his passport. Needing access to Arab countries, he held a passport which carried a stamp showing that he had been a recent visitor to Israel. He was in an awkward predicament, but he received timely advice from a friend who knew the workings of the passport office. 'It was cleverly done by somebody at the passport office in Liverpool who was a great cricket fan. I was advised to lose my passport. So I went to Liverpool and said I'd lost it. I stayed there all day while my passport and visa were sorted out for me – because I had to ask for this one man at the passport office.'

In the week leading up to departure, getting his new passport took care of Monday. On Tuesday Tommy had all his jabs. On Wednesday he was in constant touch with the TCCB, faxing through photographs and completing paperwork. It was then that he heard that Barrie Meyer would not be accompanying him. Nevertheless, the two teams, who had found much to argue about over the years, were united in demanding umpires from England as a condition for playing in what were essentially exhibition matches. The TCCB were therefore relieved that they had managed to find Basharat Hassan to replace Meyer. 'Basher' Hassan had played for Nottinghamshire for almost two decades before spending three years on the first-class umpires panel, but he had come off the list at the end of the previous summer and taken a post as commercial manager at Trent Bridge. He was ideally qualified, and fortunately he could be spared.

After an anxious weekend, and within 48 hours of when he would be leaving Bretherton, Tommy's tickets arrived. On Wednesday, 2nd September he left Heathrow on an overnight flight to Oman. He and Basher Hassan were travelling with the Pakistan team, who had just completed their tour of England. There was a minor hiccup with Tommy's luggage, the only bag in a consignment of 24 that did not have a Pakistani name. Tommy was seated with his new umpiring colleague and amongst Pakistan players that included Salim Malik, Mudassar Nazar and Javed Miandad. Though much of the conversation was in an alien tongue, Tommy picked up references to the ball tampering hiatus, but the TCCB had made it clear that he should avoid any discussion of the topic.

They arrived in Oman at 7.07, Tommy's diary records, and by nine o'clock they were breakfasting at their hotel. There was no time for acclimatisation, just a few hours rest before setting off at 1.30 for a match that was billed to start at 3.30. With the mercury at 120 degrees Fahrenheit, it was not the ideal weather for cricket. And Tommy was soon to find out that this was exactly how Javed Miandad, the Pakistan captain, felt about the matter.

The two matches that were to be played were not official ODIs, but their purpose was to celebrate the growth of the game in these newly flourishing states, where impressive stadia had recently been built and where just about anyone who was anyone was busily jumping on a bandwagon of self-promotion through association with games that involved the recently-crowned world champions of one-day cricket and their arch rivals India, who had won the title in 1983. A lavish and glossy programme billed the first match as Charms India v Majan Hotel Pakistan. They were playing for the Charms Trophy in the Muscat Cricket Challenge. The programme opened with a full colour plate of the Sultan of Oman, followed by unctuous words from the ambassadors for Pakistan and India, local dignitaries and the top brass of Oman cricket. Twenty seven thousand packed into the Baushar Stadium in the Sultan Qaboos Sports Complex to watch the match, while television cameras were waiting to beam pictures across the region. Played with white balls and black sight screens, as night fell the match enjoyed the best floodlights Tommy had seen.

This was the greatest day in Oman's cricket history. But it was too hot for Javed Miandad. The Pakistan captain made clear to the umpires that, just off a plane from London, his team were not willing to step out onto the field at the scheduled hour. The crowd had been promised a 50-over match. This would have meant a start at 3.30 with play continuing till almost midnight. And the players, like the umpires, had not been to bed in the past 36 hours. Miandad wanted a 40-over match. 'We got both captains together and Miandad was being a bit as he is – I knew him well because he had played in our league and for Sussex.' The diplomacy of Tommy and Basher Hassan managed to negotiate a contest of 45 overs a side that began at 4.30.

In the end it was a cracking game with a youthful Inzamam-ul-Haq scoring 119 in 100 balls after Pakistan's opening pair had been out for ducks – both lbw, one for each umpire. After making 247 on the artificial pitch, Pakistan just managed to restrict India's batsmen to 226 for a 21-run victory. India's reply had started with three run outs. Sachin Tendulkar then hit a sparkling 84 from 62 balls, before Waqar Younis stepped in. Bowling from Tommy's end, he dismissed Tendulkar and 43-year-old Sunil Gavaskar, who had come out of retirement for the occasion, before sweeping away the tail to finish with five for 25. Inzamam was declared

Man of the Match, but it will have been a close-run decision. For Tommy, Waqar's bowling that day was a spell to rival Mike Procter's effort back in 1979. He was amazed at the late swing the Pakistani achieved, and he was able to confirm that he had managed it without any illegal manipulation of the ball's surface.

Much was made in the press of the disgruntled Miandad's performance. He had started by deputing Mudassar Nazar to toss on his behalf. Then, batting third wicket down, he retired after facing only five balls. Returning late in the innings, he immediately threw his wicket away, and he did not take the field for the Indian innings. 'It wasn't as the papers said,' Tommy told a local reporter on his return to England. 'He told me he had a bad back, and you can't argue with that.' Now that he has less need to be diplomatic, Tommy gives his real opinion: 'He just didn't want to play.'

After the formal presentations Tommy was back at his hotel by 12.45. There were just a few hours in bed before an early call at 5.00 am to get him to the airport for the 7.00 am flight to Dubai. At the Hotel Imperial he snatched a few hours of sleep before it was time to set off for the next match. A Mercedes was laid on to take the umpires to the Al Shabab Stadium. Now billed as 'The Clash of the Titans' with the two teams styled Videocon Indian XI and Metro Milan Pakistani XI, the match was a sell-out and the Mercedes struggled through swarming crowds to one of only two entrances the authorities had chosen to open. Tommy's notebook records the temperature at 120 degrees Fahrenheit, but to local eyes it was 'pleasantly cool' and 'far easier playing in Dubai than in the pressure cooker cauldron of Sharjah.'

The fine facilities of the two stadiums in which the matches were played did not extend to the provision of umpires' changing rooms, so the umpires split up, each spending one day with a different team – a help to Tommy in catching up on some of their gossip. Mohammed Azharuddin, he heard, was being wooed by Durham. Salim Malik was put out that, when he had complained about an English umpire ignoring no balls, he had been told to shut up.

Once again there was a delayed start, this time because the Pakistan team's kit had failed to make its way from the airport to the ground, though the locally reported version of the reduction to 45 overs was that 'the players decided to let the sun go down a bit.' This time Pakistan, despite a pitch with low bounce and a slow outfield, reached 290 in their 45 overs, Inzamam again top-scoring with 92, well supported by Aamir Sohail and Moin Khan. The reply began with a slow opening stand of 91 between Kris Srikkanth and Sanjay Manjrekar. India were soon slipping well behind the required rate and the batsmen who followed threw their wickets away in pursuit of an ever more remote target, giving Pakistan a comfortable win by 99 runs.

The presentation formalities over, Tommy was able to enjoy a lie in on the Saturday before setting off for a look round Dubai's glittering shopping malls and the world famous Gold Souk. There were a few purchases for Barbara before it was time to set off for the airport and the long journey home. But before this, Basher Hassan and Tommy were beginning to wonder whether anyone might be paying them. Tommy had incurred a long list of expenses in getting down to Heathrow from Bretherton. He had been assured that all would be looked after in Dubai, but such indelicate matters are not dealt with simply in the United Arab Emirates. 'About five men came to the hotel where we were staying. "We've come to settle up with you." I think we were paid in dollars. We were quite well paid, but not as well as Inzamam when he was named Man of the Match. I think he got something like 2,500 dollars.'

The long flight back to the UK had been preceded by a shorter one to Muscat. When Tommy's plane left for London it was 1.30 am. He had expected to be in business class, as when he had travelled out, but he was befriended by Wasim Akram, already a Lancashire player. 'He was in first class, and the next thing I know he's arranged for me to sit with him. We'd both been to Gold Souk in Dubai. I'd bought Barbara a gold ring – I had it valued at about two or three hundred pounds. Wasim Akram had been shopping there too. He said, "I always buy gold." And he opened his shirt. "Have a look at this." He'd four or five chains wrapped round his neck. He just walked through customs, no bother.' Tommy had already found his own fame of some help in dealing with officialdom. 'In Dubai I was grabbed by customs. "Will you go in this room to be searched?" I thought I've got nothing to hide. So I went into this room and this man came in. He said, "Weren't you umpiring yesterday at the stadium?" I said, "Correct." He said, "I'm not bothering with you. Sit down there for a minute or two then go out!"'

Tommy dozed off as the plane made its way back. Travelling with the sun now meant that the seven-hour flight reached Heathrow at 4.00 am. He travelled north finding David Lloyd, newly appointed coach of Lancashire, on the train. By 2.15 that afternoon, he was at Preston station with Barbara to welcome him home. In the five days he had been away he calculated that he had travelled 7,274 miles. It had been a fabulous trip, yet he had barely had one proper night's sleep and how he had missed his wife's cooking. 'It was curry for lunch, curry for supper and curry for breakfast. I think I'd had enough curry!'

Chapter Eleven

Giants of minor counties cricket

Tommy's trips abroad punctuated an umpiring career in which he has stood in more minor county championship matches (at least 184) over more seasons (35, with 34 consecutively) than any other umpire. Until the late 1980s the first-class counties remained responsible for finding both umpires for all their home matches in the Second Eleven Championship, and thereafter until 2006 they continued to appoint one, whose partner would come from the first-class or reserve list. Until 2000 Tommy was always in the small pool of local umpires used by Lancashire, securing a total of 37 championship appointments, the first eight being two-day games, the remainder, from 1977, three-day fixtures. When the Lancashire Cricket Association (later the Board), have required officials for their major matches, Tommy has again been at the top of their list. In league cricket he claims 62 unbroken years of service in the white coat, a feat he believes to be unmatched nationally and one that could be of interest to the Guinness Book of Records.

For many years standing in the Minor Counties Eleven's match against the touring team was the big prize for MCCA's best umpire. Tommy has been chosen to stand on four occasions. The first was against the Pakistanis in 1982, when he was with Brian Harrison at Slough in a match spoilt by the weather that the tourists won by seven wickets. Three years later, when he stood against the Zimbabweans at Cleethorpes with Stan Levison, the three-day match was first-class. Among those who toured for a country still awaiting Test status were Andy Pycroft, now an elite match referee with the ICC, who captained the side, Dave Houghton, later to coach Derbyshire, and 19-year-old Graeme Hick, destined to transfer allegiance to England and play 65 Tests. Though the Minor Counties gained a first innings lead and the Zimbabweans looked in some danger, the match fizzled out as a dull draw, an undefeated century from Pycroft snuffing out any prospect of defeat.

For the fixture with the New Zealanders at Lakenham in 1986, a match that ended in a ten-wicket win for the touring side, Tommy was partnered by David Halfyard. It was to be the last time Tommy would stand in a first-class match. Halfyard, after the second of two spells on the first-class list, the first interrupted by his return to the game as a player, had now re-joined the MCCA list. He died ten years later, two days after officiating in his last match of the season just as plans were afoot to extend his time on the list beyond the normal retiring age of 65.

Tommy's last engagement with a full touring side came at Darlington in 1991, when he was accompanied by Gerry Stickley for a drawn two-day game against the West Indians. A Somerset chicken farmer who was on the first-class reserve list that year, Stickley was destined to join the band of those without playing credentials whose time as a top umpire was short-lived, but he has subsequently enjoyed a fruitful career as a scorer, still serving Somerset in the summer of 2014. Though two days proved inadequate to avoid the game petering out as the tamest of draws, Tommy's most salient memory is of play being interrupted when an ambulance was called and drove over the field to tend a spectator who had collapsed. Sadly, the man died. 'I won't forget the concern shown by Viv Richards and his players,' Tommy says.

From 1983, the year in which the first round of the NatWest Trophy expanded, important changes were also introduced to the Minor Counties Championship. The country was split down the middle to create an Eastern Division and a Western Division with a final, a play-off late in the season, between the winners of each division. This was initially a 55-over one-day match. In the same year the Trophy, a knock-out competition also of 55 overs a side, was introduced. The changes brought further opportunities for the most highly regarded umpires to be rewarded, and Tommy has taken charge of three one-day championship deciders and he has also been chosen to stand in three Trophy finals. The new structure also meant that Tommy's umpiring horizons broadened during the season. No longer were his appointments confined to counties in the northern half of the country. From 1983 they would be split between the two divisions and he would have opportunities to see the best cricketers from Cornwall, Devon and other minor counties from the south when they travelled to take on northern opponents.

The first of Tommy's three championship finals came in 1985, when he was with Ken Shenton at Worcester, the traditional venue for the final. There was a convincing 58-run win for Cheshire against Suffolk. Man of the Match was 46-year-old Arthur Sutton, in the penultimate year of a career for Cheshire that stretched across 28 seasons. Tommy's next two finals were with Paul Adams and the first, in 1993, was full of incident. 'Tommy always says, "You and I did loads of finals," Paul says but points out, quite correctly, that there were only two! Despite having completed his second season on the first-class reserve list, Paul still regarded it as a red letter day to stand with Tommy, already seen as a legendary figure of the minor counties game. 'For me, it was a bit like the first time I ever stood with Dickie Bird. You know, you've got the final with Tommy Wilson – oh, crikey, Tommy's been there for ever.' Paul was soon at his ease. 'Tommy's a lovely man and he was endearingly deferential to me, which was ridiculous, given the amount of cricket he's done. There was no question of I'm Tommy Wilson and I've been doing it for years and you'll go along with whatever I say – that's not in his nature at all.'

The two games were both badly affected by the weather, especially the first between Cheshire and Staffordshire. Though a one-day 55-over match was intended, a reserve day was set aside – and it was needed. Overnight Cheshire had made 66 for four and there were further delays on the Monday. Ground, weather and light issues were there to test the best of umpires. 'By this time I was on the first-class reserve list and Tommy had been round the block for 25 years, so thankfully we got it right,' Paul says. At three o'clock they felt it was still not suitable for play, but they got the captains together and, applying the laws as they then stood, suggested that they went away and discussed the matter, making clear that play would resume only if both agreed.

The match re-started and Staffordshire were eventually required to make 175 in their 55 overs. A Cheshire team that included Geoff Miller, once of England, and Tony Murphy, formerly an opening bowler for Lancashire and Surrey, were soon on top. Five wickets were down for 40 and few would have bet against a Cheshire win, but Simon Myles, who had played a few games for Warwickshire, and his skipper, Paul Newman, formerly of Derbyshire, knuckled down. The stand prospered, but it was mid-September and the light was fading fast. Paul remembers going to Tommy and asking if they should offer the light. Tommy agreed that they should. This was an offer Staffordshire could not afford to accept. The minimum number of overs to constitute a match had passed, they were behind the asking rate and going off would have handed Cheshire the match.

The light worsened, but the two batsmen had their eyes in. As Newman defended, Myles went for his shots. 'He played out of his skin,' Paul remembers. Suddenly the inevitability of a Cheshire win was no more. The laws provided no chance to offer the light to the fielding side and Cheshire captain Ian Cockbain, once of Lancashire, realised this. 'He was brilliant,' Paul says, '"Come on, we're not going off. The umpires are right." The whole thing was superb.' Against all odds the batting side reached their target without losing another wicket, Myles ending on 94.

The second final in which Tommy and Paul stood together came two years later, in 1995. This match would have completed a hat-trick of finals for Paul and Tommy, had Tommy not been forced to withdraw in 1994 when he was having trouble with his right knee. He was nevertheless able to be on the ground that year to receive an inscribed tankard to mark his 25 years of umpiring in MCCA cricket.

For the 1995 final Devon and Lincolnshire travelled to Worcester. For Tommy it brought one of the most intriguing characters in his minor counties experience, Peter Roebuck. To die in tragic and never fully-explained circumstances in South Africa in 2011, Roebuck had come to minor counties cricket after winning a blue at Cambridge and spending a further 15 years with Somerset, three of them as captain. After one season with Devon, he took over the captaincy, while his cricket acquired a new dimension with his emergence as a crafty spin bowler, evidenced by an amazing return of nine for 12 against Oxfordshire.

In 1994 there had been an attempt at making the final a two-innings match over the usual two days, but it ended in a tame draw; so in 1995 the one-day format returned, again with a spare day but with the overs reduced to 50. Once again the match provided the umpires with testing weather conditions. Put in to bat, Devon reached 170 for one at the end of a shortened first day. Next day, the captains cooperated in agreeing the resumption. Devon then progressed to 263 for two, a total that they defended successfully to win by 57 runs.

In conversation with Ken Shenton, Tommy reflects on the complex character that was Peter Roebuck. A brilliant captain and a strong personality, they both agree, but not one to suffer fools. 'He was a scholar and a sportsman. He was always thinking about the game. He was almost two overs ahead of you in what he was going to do,' Ken says. Tommy remembers that 'he set the field and whoever bowled in his team bowled to that field. He went wild if they didn't.' Yet this same, intense man could be a child at heart, 'racing down the motorway at 100 miles an hour in a silly hat.' Then they recall that when mandatory samples were required for drug testing it was Roebuck who refused. 'He was told he'd be out of the game if he didn't do it.'

When the Minor Counties Trophy began in 1983 Tommy was chosen for the first final. He stood with Don Norton at Macclesfield, where Cheshire, who included a young Mike Watkinson, beat Bedfordshire by 36 runs. Three years later he was with David Halfyard at St Albans, where they saw Norfolk beat Hertfordshire by 30 runs. The following year he and Clive Smith stood at Christ Church, Oxford, where Cheshire were again successful, beating Cambridgeshire by eight wickets.

All these finals had featured some of the herculean figures of the minor counties game. In a career that spanned two world wars, running from 1907 to 1946, Michael Falcon played 247 championship matches for Norfolk, a figure since exceeded by only one man, Harry Henderson, Northumberland wicket-keeper, with 255. Perhaps Falcon still stands alone on the podium of greatness in the minor counties game, but Oxfordshire's Mike Nurton, the championship's highest run-maker, has clocked up 242 matches, while Cheshire's Arthur Sutton with 239 is close behind. Like Falcon, Sutton was an all-rounder, one of only ten batsmen with over 10,000 championship runs and, with 437 victims, his county's leading wicket-taker. Others with well over 100 championship matches for their counties who have played in one of Tommy's six finals include: Steve Dean and Mark Humphries (Staffordshire), Ian Cockbain, Bob Cooke and Neil O'Brien (Cheshire), Phil Caley (Suffolk), Nick Gaywood (Devon), Frank Collyer, Alan Garofall and Tim Smith (Hertfordshire), Mark Fell (Lincolnshire), Nigel Gadsby (Cambridgeshire), Fred Handley, Robin Huggins, Doug Mattocks and Steve Plumb (Norfolk).

Challenged to pick a team from those who played during his time on the MCCA list, Tommy set to work. Though over half the team he wanted had been respected skippers of their counties, he had no hesitation in naming the captain of his side. For Tommy, none quite matched Peter Roebuck. 'People would play for him because they admired him as a player – batsman, bowler and cricket tactician. He could set a field and when he had set that field – "a bit wider at leg gully – now make a mark there" – he expected his fielders to bowl to it.' A martinet he may have been, but Roebuck still played the game as Tommy would wish, graciously accepting the correctness of an lbw decision when he was on 98 in a match at Alderley Edge. But is Tommy's choice strictly eligible after Roebuck's long and distinguished time with Somerset? No, disallowed! We agreed to concentrate on those whose career was primarily in minor county cricket. This ruled out David Ward, otherwise a certain choice with his 20 centuries in 75 matches for Hertfordshire, and former Test players such as Derek Randall, Graham Roope and Mudassar Nazar could not be considered. So who replaces the cerebral Roebuck? 'It has to be Arthur Sutton,' says Tommy. 'He had the respect of his players. He was a good captain. He knew the opposition and how to get their batsmen out. And he wasn't frightened of declaring and setting a realistic total that would tempt the other side into losing their wickets.'

Spoilt for choice with opening batsmen, Tommy opts for Steve Dean of Staffordshire, whom he sees as the most accomplished player never to have graced the first-class game, while the solidity of Mike Nurton over so many years makes him the ideal partner for Dean. He acknowledges the case for Malcolm Roberts of Buckinghamshire, with 16 hundreds in just 76 matches, but Roberts, like many others from southern counties, was a player Tommy seldom saw at first hand. Those who played for Cumberland, Cheshire and Staffordshire had more chance to impress, and one vying for the opener's spot was Bob Entwistle, who played 91 matches for Cumberland when his days fighting vainly for a spot in the Lancashire side came to an end. Entwistle is to bat at three, and his selection is reinforced by his fearless fielding on the edge of the popping crease at short leg. 'No shin guards, no arm guards, nothing,' says Tommy, 'but they didn't get much past him.'

At four will be Nick Folland, the left-hander whose runs for Devon came at an average of over 50 and earned a contract with Somerset that lasted just two summers before he chose to return to the cricket he loved best. 'A marvellous player,' says Tommy, 'and a fine stroke player able to capitalise on the solid start I'm expecting to get from my top three. He was one who never queried a decision. You gave him out and off he went.'

Ian Cockbain, Nick Gaywood and Neil Riddell of Durham are among those whose claims Tommy found hard to resist, but there is another old-style gentleman of minor counties cricket and a fine adaptable batsman for whom he must find a place, Steve Plumb of Norfolk and later of Lincolnshire. 'He could batten down the hatches or attack.' Tommy has a soft spot for Norfolk. 'I remember umpiring them at Jesmond and we umpires were invited to join the Norfolk side for a dinner they'd arranged at the club for the evening of the first day.'

At six will be the captain Sutton, to be followed by another all-rounder, Steve Greensword. Briefly with Leicestershire, he began a 26-year minor county career with Durham, for whom he played 154 matches before moving to Northumberland, where he extended his tally by a further 52. 'Another very tough competitor,' says Tommy, speaking of a man who went on to become an umpire of distinction though turning too late to officiating to be considered for the minor counties list.

To keep wicket Tommy has weighed up the claims of Frank Collyer, Tommy Hodson and Mark Humphries, but his choice is a man he has regularly seen at close quarters in his long career with Cumberland, Simon Dutton. Also a handy batsman, Dutton passed a century on three occasions for his county and also enjoyed a spell as captain. Ruling out Roebuck has left Tommy's team bereft of spinners, and it is to left-armer Ken Norton of Northumberland that he turns, just ahead of Peter Kippax, the leg spinner from Durham and Malcolm Woods of Cumberland, with his off-breaks delivered in the manner of a right-arm Derek Underwood, while Tommy acknowledges sadly that he has seen too little of Peter Lewington of Berkshire, whose off breaks brought him over 600 wickets at less than 19 each.

Turning to his opening bowlers, Doug Yeabsley in a 29-year career captured 735 wickets at just over 20 each for Devon. But, at 43 years of age, he was past his best when Tommy first saw him in action, though still good enough to take six Cheshire wickets for 36 that day. With David Halfyard ruled out as too well established in first-class cricket, Tommy chooses David Halliwell from Cumberland and Keith Arnold of Oxfordshire. 'On his day Halliwell was as quick as anyone I knew in minor county cricket, but his biggest problem was running down the track. Arnold was a good pace too. His biggest problem was no balling. Both were ferocious appealers.'

And what about a twelfth man? 'We'll have Phil Caley of Suffolk,' says Tommy, adding that the current chairman of the MCCA cricket committee would be a good man to have around. 'He was a very good player, for sure. And if we put him in, he might buy the book,' Tommy adds with a characteristic chuckle.

Championship statistics for the chosen team are shown below:

	Matches	Runs	Average	Wickets	Average
S.J. Dean	161	10,163	38.20		
M.D. Nurton	242	12,684	33.20		
R. Entwistle	91	5,708	39.09		
N.A. Folland	145	10,321	51.86		
S.G. Plumb	189	12,266	41.86	335	31.62
J.A. Sutton	239	10,577	28.50	437	20.23
S. Greensword	206	8,684	32.52	464	20.60
S.M. Dutton	119	4,163			
D. Halliwell	59	723	18.07	222	21.61
K.A. Arnold	209	1,292	11.23	688	22.64
K. Norton	220	414	6.08	599	21.00

Chapter Twelve

An old dog learning new tricks

In Tommy's long umpiring career, he has seen many changes to the traditional game that was played almost universally in the 1950s. Among these has been the introduction of the Duckworth Lewis (D/L) method to limited overs cricket. Before the start of the 1998 season there was a compulsory session for umpires to explain how D/L worked. Tommy was first confronted with the need to apply it in July of that summer. He and Ken Shenton were at Wellington for a Trophy quarter-final between Shropshire and Lincolnshire. Frank Duckworth and Tony Lewis, co-inventors of the mathematical formulae that addressed the challenge of maintaining a fair contest in an interrupted match, were by their telephones, Duckworth assigned to Tommy's match. The early days of D/L stretched the intellects of several commentators, who struggled to get to grips with a concept that sought to compensate batting sides for the loss of one of cricket's two scoring resources – balls still to be bowled, while taking note of the other resource, wickets still in hand, at the time of the break. Sometimes to the layman the revised targets appeared illogical or unfair, and those to whom the inner workings of their car or computer could happily remain a mystery demanded to understand the maths of D/L.

Among the uncomprehending doubters at Wellington was Neville Birch, a former minor counties umpire now charged with the duties of competitions secretary for the MCCA. If Tommy had had any problems with D/L, he had Frank Duckworth awaiting his call, but he knew he could rely on Barbara to get the calculations right, just as she would later assist him by noting time lost for injuries or lost balls when he might have had to impose penalties for slow over rates in his role as match referee. 'Come to lunch and talk me through it,' Birch suggested to Barbara. 'I can't talk you through it in ten minutes,' Barbara protested, 'it's a big job.'

These were the days before the system became more sophisticated with computers to do the calculations. 'We had it on postcards,' Tommy remembers. 'Barbara was on the boundary doing the maths. She worked it out, then we went to the captains and I told them what it was. The chap from Lincolnshire went berserk. Neville said, "This is ridiculous – we're going to ring David Armstrong."' Ignoring the chance to ring Frank Duckworth, a call was duly put through. Armstrong's reply was uncompromising. 'Ken Shenton and Tommy Wilson, whatever they say goes,' the MCCA secretary said. 'They understand it. I don't.' The Lincolnshire captain had not been the only one incandescent at how the D/L formula appeared to be working against his team. Tommy remembers the county's chairman, a large bearded man whom they all called Rumpole of the Bailey. 'He went berserk with me and Ken because he didn't understand it.' The tantrums were all to no avail. The intricacies of how the targets needed to be adjusted that day are lost in the sands of time, but Tommy remains certain that the formula was applied correctly. Lincolnshire used only 45 of their original allocation of 60 overs in scoring 173. Shropshire then knocked off the runs for the loss of three wickets in 36 overs with the former Warwickshire player Asif Din undefeated on 94.

Asked to pick out some of the special moments he has encountered over the years of minor counties and second eleven umpiring, Tommy mentions a match from 1984 when Lancashire Second Eleven played Derbyshire at Blackpool. Batting first, Derbyshire scored 173 and looked well placed when their attack, led by a still inexperienced Devon Malcolm, reduced the home team to 53 for six. Opener David Varey, a Cambridge blue, was still at the wicket, 24 not out. The clock showed 5.02 when skipper Harry Pilling joined him. At 6.40 the following day the stand ended, when Pilling was out for 181, by which time they had added 423 with Varey undefeated on 244. Lancashire went on to win by an innings and 58 runs.

Tommy then cites one of the most remarkable matches in the annals of the minor counties: Cumberland v Cambridgeshire in 1987. He particularly recalls that the winning captain reputedly gave him and fellow umpire Ken Shenton no marks for their efforts. Originally scheduled to be played at Barrow, the match was transferred to Penrith, where the umpires had still considered the ground unsuitable for the match to start. However, at that time they could be overruled by the captains, who were both keen to get going. A strong Cambridgeshire team included four former first-class cricketers, among them Stuart Turner, once of Essex. On winning the toss, they decided to field and bowled Cumberland out for 96, of which Steven Sharp made 54. Conditions still favoured the bowlers as Cambridgeshire in reply made only 122, Turner contributing 45. The innings lasted one ball short of 24 overs, and Ken Shenton remembers a 20-year-old opening bowler Philip Threlfall, later to play three first-class matches for Sussex, trying to bowl too fast for the conditions. He took three early wickets but ended with figures of 8 – 1 – 55 – 3. Turner then gave him a lesson in how to make best use of the damp pitch. 'He found all he had to do was put it on the spot.'

Cumberland were dismissed for 47, Turner returning figures of 13.3 – 10 – 11 – 10, the finest analysis ever recorded in the Minor Counties Championship. Under a new regulation introduced that year, an extra hour of play was permitted if a result was possible, and this allowed Cambridgeshire to try to knock off the 22 runs needed that evening. In 4.5 overs they hit 25 without loss, Threlfall now managing to concede 23 of the runs in 17 balls. But when this brief passage of play had been interrupted by rain, the two umpires had taken the players off the field. Had they not been able to return, both teams would have been obliged to come back to the ground the following day. 'The Cambridge captain marked us nought each,' Tommy remembers. 'We knew that because the Cumberland captain came to us rather embarrassed to tell us that he wasn't the one that had marked us down.'

A complete revision of the Laws of Cricket heralded a new code that came into effect in October 2000. Perhaps the most revolutionary innovation was bringing in penalty runs for a range of offences that had hitherto been limited to illegal fielding. To Tommy the new provisions came as a welcome sanction available to umpires, hitherto powerless to take action when plagued by batsmen who were reluctant to run off the pitch. He remembers an instance a few years before the new law had come in when he was officiating an England Under 19 trial match with Brian Harrison. Tommy had become exasperated with the running of a young Gareth Batty and shared his feelings with his colleague. Harrison then took up his position at the bowler's end. A characteristic of Harrison's umpiring was taking his time over his decisions, commonly sticking his thumbs under his coat as though wearing a waistcoat before bending forward and bringing his finger up. There was an appeal for lbw, but the batsmen ran as Harrison went through his deliberation procedure. 'He stands there like this and he brings his finger up. "Thou'll not run down that pitch no more. Thou's out. Go!" Then he turns to me at square leg. "Wilson, if you want to know owt about umpiring, ask a master. That's the way to stop 'em running on t' pitch. Get rid of 'em!"'

It was not long before Tommy availed himself of the new powers to impose penalty runs. An England Under 19 batsman found he had cost his side five runs when Tommy ruled that that he had run on the pitch once too often in a match at Scarborough. 'The England Under 19 scorer came running out of the box: "I don't understand the penalty runs. There's nothing in my book."' Tommy took similar action against the fielding side in a semi-final of the 38-County Cup in 2002, and he proudly claims to have been the first umpire to award penalty runs at Old Trafford. 'They didn't understand what penalty runs were either!'

In 2001, the first season of the new laws, penalty runs had not been applied in the first-class game and many other competitions were reluctant to embrace them, especially where unqualified umpires were likely to be standing. Tommy quickly became used to having the sanction available to him in the Northern League, but instances of penalties being applied across the country were rare and confusion always threatened if an umpire chose to impose the law. That year, Tommy was chosen to stand in the final of the National Club Championship at Lord's, where Bramhall were to play Bath. His partner was Welsh umpire Steve Kuhlmann. Frank Kemp, ECB's Cricket Operations Manager (Recreational), was on the ground and sought out the two umpires. His message was a simple one: 'I've just come to make sure that we won't have any penalty runs today. I don't want penalty runs at Lord's.'

Kemp's instructions were awkward for the umpires, and he was exceeding his authority in suggesting what would have been a change to the match regulations. It was a wet day and Tommy was soon doing his duty: 'I warned the two batsmen for running up and down on the pitch. Then Steve gave them a final warning. And I'm stood there thinking please don't run down the track – Kemp doesn't want penalty runs.' The batsmen let Tommy off – he was spared the wrath of Kemp as the match was settled with a boundary off the final ball to give Bramhall a four-wicket win.

Among the many prestigious matches in which Tommy has stood few were more special than his first appointment at Wormsley, the beautiful ground in Buckinghamshire created by the late Sir John Paul Getty. In 2002 Tommy accompanied Don Oslear for a match in which Sir Paul's XI played an MCCA team.

Don Oslear and Tommy
at Wormsley

Sir Paul was to die the following year and Tommy remembers that when the frail old man came to watch the match, he was in a wheelchair with six bodyguards in attendance. 'I'll never forget when they arrived. There was a big black car followed by another big black car. Six men jumped out and surrounded Sir John Paul, who was sat in his wheelchair. They made themselves inconspicuous but nobody was going to shoot John Paul Getty – that was for certain.' This match gave MCCA chairman John Pickup the opportunity to make a post-match presentation of a Wisden to Tommy to mark his 34 years of minor counties umpiring. In 2009 he was in Pickup's county to stand in an MCCA match at Chester Boughton Hall to mark 100 years of Cheshire cricket.

Tommy's other important appointments have included many age group matches. The biggest of these came in 1999 when he stood in the match between England Under 18 and Australia Under 19, seeing at first hand the rising talent of Michael Clarke and Mitchell Johnson, while other age group matches have given Tommy the chance to officiate players too numerous to list who have gone on to represent their country, among them Andrew Flintoff. When Flintoff led the England Under 19 Eleven against Durham University, there were seven future Test players in his side. These appointments have also led to Tommy's proud claim that he has stood at some level in a match involving all the Test-playing nations with the exception of Sri Lanka, and he was denied a full house only when he broke his leg shortly before he was due to stand in a match involving the Sri Lankan Under 19 side in 2000.

In 2004 came a memorable match for Tommy, in which he was appointed with John Tythcott to umpire a three-day match at Sleaford between the ECB Development of Excellence XI and the Under 19 team from Bangladesh. Tommy was standing at square leg when a Bangladeshi, batting with increasing freedom on his way to a big hundred, hooked a ball in his direction. A fielder attempted to take the catch but could only divert the ball onto Tommy's forehead. Dazed and with his head swollen up 'like a huge egg', Tommy was forced to leave the field for treatment by the England physio. An ice-filled muslin stocking was placed over his head to ease the swelling. The treatment completed, Tommy claimed he was fit to return to the field. 'So the physio put a new lot on and I put my cap on over it.' Tommy returned, replacing the Bangladeshis' Australian coach, who had been standing in at square leg. 'John Tythcott said, "I've taught them a song. They'll sing it to you in a bit."' It was a hot day, but just after Tommy had resumed his position, he had the impression it was starting to drizzle. 'But it was the sun that had melted the ice and I was absolutely wet through. A wicket fell, then John goes, "Come on, sing for Tommy."' The players duly struck up together. 'There's only one Tommy Wilson' they all began to chant.

Two weeks later Tommy was a guest of ECB at Sophia Gardens in Cardiff for the third of the Bangladesh team's three-Test series against the England Under 19 side, which was captained by Alastair Cook. Seeing Tommy on the committee balcony, the Bangladesh players, many of whom spoke little English, took advantage of a drinks break to assemble on the boundary edge in front of the pavilion. There they gave a second rendition of the Sleaford song. Most of those on the committee balcony were bemused by what was happening, but the singing of the Bangladeshi boys that day ensured that, from then on, his umpiring friends would all know that 'there's only one Tommy Wilson.'

In 2002 Tommy had imagined he had stood in his last championship game, but two years later he answered an emergency call and joined Mike Dixon for an encore of his swansong. A magnificent game of cricket saw Graham Lloyd finish with an undefeated 90 as Cumberland beat Cambridgeshire by four wickets. It was an innings that revealed cricket's contrasting fortunes: in the first innings Lloyd had made a duck – given lbw by Tommy. His days of minor county umpiring over, a new role emerged for Tommy. The MCCA had decided that they should follow the modern trend by appointing a match referee for their championship decider. Tommy was chosen for the match between Northumberland and Cheshire at Jesmond in 2007. After years of being a one-day encounter, from 1999 it had been a two-innings match over three days, but in 2008, when Tommy was again referee, four days were allowed for the first time when Berkshire played Lincolnshire at Newbury.

Among the many ECB initiatives for grass roots cricket has been the introduction of national age group competitions for boys and girls. Tommy had earlier been involved with umpiring English Schools Association matches, from which he retains scorecards with such names as Joe Root, James Taylor and Ben Stokes playing Under 14 cricket. His love of umpiring younger cricketers was further rewarded when he took on the responsibility for appointing umpires for games at Loughborough National Cricket Centre, now the Elite Player Development Centre, where his good friend and former Lancashire player John Abrahams has been in charge of the England Under 19 team. Among the umpires Tommy appointed from those who had passed the age limit for the first-class list were Alan Whitehead, John Hampshire and Ray Julian. Not all retired umpires choose to continue standing in cricket at this level, but some are great enthusiasts for seeing the rising generation at close quarters. Ray Julian is one who has always delighted in taking lower level matches. 'When they asked the 24 on the first-class panel who would like to do second eleven, only about six hands used to go up. Mine always did!'

A more recent initiative from the ACO has been the launching of their Young Officials. Restricted to those under the age of 25, this new group embraces many young umpires still in their teens with ambitions to go as far as they can in the game. All the umpires now chosen for the finals of the Under 15 and Under 13 National Club Championships and for the Under 15 County Cup are recruited exclusively from the Young Officials. A league format for the finals provides each county with several matches. They take place at a central venue, usually a school like Oundle or Oakham, giving the umpires plenty of opportunity to show their ability. Tommy, with a little help from a few others, observes and mentors them.

The programme for the ACO's 2014 National Conference listed on one page senior umpires who earned appointments for the finals of the Royal London Club Championship, the BUCS finals, the Over 50s County Championship and other matches of comparable importance. On the next page were the names of 12 of ACO's Young Officials who were appointed to the ESCA Bunbury Cup and to the age group finals mentioned above. In alphabetical order they were: Daniel Brennan, Paddy Brown, Jonathan Crabtree, Ben Cousins, Chris Fortune, Tom Heenan, Nathan Hewitt, Sam Hollingshead, David Matthews, Jordan Montgomery-Else, Sam Stringfellow and David Tooth.

It will be a surprise and disappointment to Tommy if one or two of these names are not soon seen at the top of recreational umpiring or higher. Asked to pick a couple who particularly impressed him, Tommy opts for Paddy Brown from Lancashire and Nathan Hewitt from Notts. He points also to Alasdair Shaikh, who has progressed through the system to become, in 2013, the first young official to find a place on the full MCCA list, though Tommy admits that he and Nick Cousins may have been responsible for rushing him up the ladder a bit too quickly.

Knowing they are being closely watched and assessed could make the youngsters nervous, but Ben Cousins (unrelated to Nick), one who has done well in the matches, finds that this is not the case. Ben warmed to Tommy and his endless stories, finding that in observing he deals less in criticism than encouragement. 'He was so easy to get along with, a relaxed person to be around.' Ben adds that 'just watching him, especially before a match, how he reacts with the players was something we could all learn from.'

Though Tommy has for some years played a less prominent role as a classroom tutor of umpires, his reputation is still second to none. So it was to Tommy that David Lloyd, Lancashire's captain in that first Roses match, turned when his son Graham began to show an interest in umpiring. 'I want Tommy to train our Graham to get onto the first-class list,' he told Barbara. This was the start of some personal tutoring that Tommy gave to Graham to supplement what he was already learning at a course he was attending in Blackburn. Each week Tommy would send ten or twenty questions to Graham, wait for the homework to come back then send the answers, later encouraging Graham to mark his own paper.

After 15 years with Lancashire and winning six ODI caps, Graham Lloyd had continued playing for Bootle in the Liverpool Premier League and for Cumberland. Tommy remembers going to watch a club match, where he was observing one of the umpires. Graham Lloyd, fielding on the boundary, was curious to know what brought Tommy to the ground. Told his purpose, he replied to Tommy, 'Do you know I often watch umpires. I never say anything to them. I never question their decisions, but I watch them.' Thus was Graham Lloyd taking on board Tommy's advice as he prepared for a career that would see him rise to the first-class reserve list by 2010 and move onto the full first-class panel in 2014.

Those who have come across Tommy mentoring younger officials or in one of the many other roles he has taken up in the cause of umpiring may easily believe that his days in the middle are long past. Making clear that this is far from the truth was a full-page photograph in the July 2014 issue of The Cricketer, later used on the front cover of the ACO Newsletter, showing Tommy as the umpire for the return to cricket of Freddie Flintoff. Without a first-class match in five years, Flintoff determined to make a come-back for Lancashire in the NatWest T20 Blast. But, first of all, he needed some match practice – and where better than in a Northern Premier League match for his old club St Annes, where he had learnt his cricket as a boy?

The match, against Penrith, took place at St Annes-on-Sea on 31st May. Tommy was partnered by his old minor counties colleague Ken Shenton and inevitably the press descended, belittling the status of the game with talk of 'lowly club cricket'. Tommy knew better. He had seen the former England all-rounder from his earliest days playing age group cricket in Lancashire, and he vouches for the serious intent of Flintoff that day and his commitment to his team's cause. 'He started my end and he said, "All I've bowled up to now, Tommy, is nets. I'm going to bowl as fast as I can and if I get close to the line, you tell me. And if I bowl a no ball, call it." I said, "You needn't tell me. I will!"'

There were three wickets for Flintoff at a cost 26 in 12 overs. His second spell was from Ken's end, where Paul Hindmarch, a tall Unicorns player and the Penrith professional, was facing and fancied himself to cart the bowling out of sight. Ken remembers him drilling a ball straight back. 'I thought I'm a goner,' he admits, now able to smile. 'Flintoff saved me from death. I couldn't believe how he just plucked the ball out of the air.' For The Cricketer it was 'a nonchalant caught and bowled' that compensated for a disappointingly brief innings when Flintoff came to bat. For the two umpires it was a memorable day completed by Flintoff's demeanour off the field. 'He was there for hours signing autographs. He was a great credit to the game.'

Tommy umpiring Andrew Flintoff, St Annes, 2014

Chapter Thirteen

Observing, assessing and appointing

Tommy's standing in the umpiring world, the time at his disposal after retirement with the closing of the shop in 1995 and above all his passion for the game ensured that there would be a continuing clamour for his services. One who has known Tommy well for many years is Alan Wilson. Until 2014 president of the MCCA, his playing career had been with Netherfield in the Northern League and for Cumberland, whom he captained in minor counties cricket for several years. When he became chairman of cricket for the MCCA in 1996, Alan Wilson turned to Tommy for assistance. 'Every year there was a tampering with the rules and regulations. I was the one that got Tommy involved with that. It was right up his street, and he was extremely conscientious.' Since that time Tommy has become ever more involved with the MCCA and everything that pertains to its umpiring as well as being widely used by other bodies.

Until 2007 the training and grading of recreational umpiring throughout the UK, but not the first-class game, had been coordinated by the ACU&S, the organisation first set up by Tom Smith back in 1953. This essentially amateur body with minimal paid support had run into difficulties. Financial problems loomed and questions were asked about the governance of the organisation. Some felt that for too long there had been a self-serving clique at the top. In Tommy's view, 'It was a closed shop. The ordinary members had no say.' Many believed that the association should be wound up and the whole business of the registration, training and development of umpires should pass to domestic cricket's governing body, the ECB. This would have brought British umpiring into line with most overseas countries, but a vocal proportion of the umpires felt a loyalty to ACU&S and spoke up for the value of having affairs under the wing of a body that was totally independent of other interests.

There was much ill feeling, never more clearly demonstrated than when an AGM was planned for Derby. It was scheduled for a Saturday in late March 2007. Past AGM attendances had always been modest with grass roots members finding little of interest to persuade them to travel up to London or wherever the meeting might have been held. Now it was different. Busloads of disaffected members descended on Derby, only to find that the room booked for the meeting could not come close to coping with the number of people wishing to attend. The floor might not have borne the weight of all who were battling to get in, while fire regulations would certainly have been seriously breached. The chief executive of Derbyshire CCC had no option but to forbid the meeting taking place.

'We were queueing outside six deep,' Tommy recalls, 'and what annoyed me was that it was a lovely day and we could all have sat in the stands. They could have rigged up microphones. That's what annoyed me about the hierarchy of the ACU&S – they all went filing past us and went into that room and announced to all and sundry that the meeting had been cancelled.' Tommy's idea of using the stands was prompted by remembering that this was how the Northern League had overcome a similar problem when there had been an accidental double booking of a venue. Whatever the practicalities of transferring to the stands, hundreds of disaffected members had wasted their time and money on an entirely fruitless journey. For the open-minded, such credibility as the ACU&S might still have had was fast evaporating.

A white knight was needed. A splinter group under the name IBIS, centred around Liverpool and north Wales and with minor counties umpire Mike Dixon much involved, offered one escape route and broke away entirely, but the organisation never attracted serious numbers and soon withered. The way was clear for the ECB to seize the initiative, but ECB's wish had been to take over umpiring and run it in the manner in which it ran coaching. An official body emerged with the title ECBOA, the last two letters denoting Officials Association. This was anathema to those who still clung to the ACU&S and the concept of independence and there was a danger of the umpiring fraternity being split in two. A steering group was formed under the ECB's Frank Kemp with representatives of the ACU&S to try to hold it together. There was a need for constructive thinkers and peacemakers, and Tommy was invited onto this group, while first-class umpires were represented by Peter Willey, their chairman. Illustrating the great divide between umpires on the county circuit and the rest at that time, Willey met Tommy in the Long Room at Lord's and admitted his ignorance of the grass roots association. 'I am not well versed in what it is,' he said. The outcome of the group's deliberations was the formation of the ECB ACO, the Association of Cricket Officials, the organisation coordinating umpiring affairs today with greater independence from the ECB, but still enjoying the financial security that comes from being beneath the umbrella of domestic cricket's governing body. An early ECB move was to join their first-class umpires to the new organisation as honorary members.

There were many challenges facing the new body, but before long a new professionalism was shining through and there was a vision for the future. An early appointment was of Nick Cousins as Education Manager. With a background in teaching, he came with strong cricketing credentials, having played a few second eleven games for Gloucestershire, but his crucial experience was in rugby, where he had been heavily involved with the grading and appointment of referees. Cousins quickly engaged with county ACOs in setting up a new training regime for umpires. There were revamped examinations and the concept of assessing officials from the boundary edge, long-established in rugby, was introduced. When a chief executive was sought for the ACO, Cousins was appointed. Reporting to a board chaired by former MCC chief executive and secretary Roger Knight, he oversaw the implementation of his plans, while slickly presented annual conferences held at Lord's enabled the wider membership to understand why moving on from the ACU&S was to the benefit of umpires at all levels.

'Now each county has its own county performance officer and its own county appointments officer,' Tommy explains, contrasting the ACO to the closed shop that had characterised the ACU&S. 'Now every county has the same, then you've got a regional appointments officer.' Performance data is fed up the chain and umpires at the top of ACO's eight thousand members are rewarded with appointments to such matches as the later stages of the village and club knock-out competitions and, where appropriate, fast-tracked towards the higher echelons of the game. Boundary observations and formal assessments have been a pivotal feature in ensuring that the best officials are identified and appointed to the matches they deserve.

In 2006 Chris Kelly, a former minor counties umpire with whom Tommy once stood, joined the ECB. Kelly had worked for four years as Umpires and Referees Manager with the ICC before assuming a similar role administering umpires throughout English and Welsh first-class cricket. The practice of counties appointing both umpires for their second eleven games had already eased, with a local man accompanied by one from the first-class or reserve list. Kelly now took this process one step further by bringing in what is known as the D List, some 70 umpires from whom appointments are made, through Kelly, for all county second eleven competitions and other matches of comparable importance for which the ECB is responsible. Needing to know who the best umpires were, Kelly enlisted a small group of experienced umpires to observe and report back on the performance of those aspiring to move up the ladder and gain appointment to the reserve list for the first-class game. While the assessment process is designed to play an important part in the training of umpires further down the ladder, few were better qualified to carry out these duties at the highest level than Tommy, who was one of Kelly's first appointments together with retired

Test umpire Don Oslear, Paul Adams and Dave Burden, one of the doyens of minor county officiating.

Kelly now works principally with Paul Adams, and it is they who decide each year who should be added to the D list and who should be removed from it. For the most highly regarded, and especially those with playing experience at the top level, there can be promotion to the ECB Emerging Umpires List, just four names in 2014, who become the primary candidates for promotion to the reserve list and thence, perhaps, into the first-class game. Tommy, meanwhile, has been switched to organising assessments for ACO and the MCCA, undertaking some himself and assigning others to qualified assessors around the country. One year he ensured that every umpire on the MCCA list was observed and reported upon. Then he concentrated on those on the reserve list. Now he intends to switch his principal focus: 'We're going to be looking at and finding out about, mentoring if you will, the ones that have been suggested as the next group of umpires looking to come onto minor counties – find out how they're getting on in different leagues, talking to different coaches and captains about them.'

How does Tommy set about the task? And what does he feel he can learn from the boundary edge? He draws a distinction between the lowest level (Level 1a in ECO terminology), where the newly qualified umpire has just passed his first exam, and higher up the chain. Low level assessment may be in the hands of an on-field colleague, whose match duties inevitably limit the extent to which he can watch his partner. Where an outside assessor is conducting the observation at Levels 1a and 2, the normal procedure would be for the umpire to be notified in advance, and for the assessor to introduce himself before the start of the match. Level 3, which can take an able umpire a couple of years to pass, is the pathway towards the first-class list. These high level assessments are principally the responsibility of Hughie Evans with Tommy closely involved. The umpires being watched will have been recommended by their county performance officers and may already be on the MCCA panel or the D list. In such cases the assessor comes incognito, but he may break cover if he chooses to look at the pitch in the tea interval, as Tommy would, to see how effective the umpire has been in keeping bowlers off the protected area of the pitch.

For a Level 2 assessment Tommy's practice is to be at the ground an hour in advance. He likes to see the umpire arrive. How smartly dressed is he? 'If he's in a pair of jeans and an old sweater, I mark him down.' He likes to see his pre-match preparation, watch how he familiarises himself with the boundaries and any ground peculiarities, how he introduces himself to the captains, how he is dressed at the time of the toss (he should not yet be in his white coat). Less importance attaches to such matters at Level 3, but for a two- or three-day match a raft of other issues require attention: observing match timings, overnight covering of the pitch, second day mowing and rolling etc.

As the match progresses, the assessor keeps his eyes trained on the umpire. Tommy is the first to admit that he is unlikely to be able to comment constructively on the correctness of most decisions in the middle, especially in the higher reaches of the game, but he develops a feel for when an umpire is giving way to player pressure, sometimes confirmed by the players. 'Some umpires make a mistake and they try to put it right. Oh, I've blundered there. Next minute, big appeal, same bowler and he gives him out – but he's not out! I'm not talking generally, but you get that with one or two umpires. They try to put things right. You've slipped up, forget it – you've made a mistake. Put it to the back of your mind because two or three captains have said to me, "Tom, over three days you'll make a mistake. I'm not bothered about one mistake. What we're looking for is consistency in decision making throughout the three days." You'll slip up once, you'll give someone lb and he's nicked it. You'll do it and they'll forget that if generally your other decisions are good.'

If decisions may often be best judged by captains' reports, there is a welter of other factors that must be considered in conducting an official assessment – and there is a comprehensive ACO form to assist the assessor. A précis of the main points covered gives a flavour of its contents: concentration, appropriate levels of intervention, fieldcraft techniques, positioning, speed of movement into position, clarity of calls, composure and ability to resist pressure, accurate application of the laws and regulations, consistency of decision making, interaction with the captain and players, dealing with ground, weather and light issues, authority and how well respected by the players, not influenced by players, officials or spectators, control of emotions, not afraid to make unpopular decisions, teamwork with colleague and scorers, eye contact and pre-arranged signalling with colleague, appropriate consultation with colleague, sharing responsibility, effective signals.

It is Tommy's view that an effective assessment is a whole-day job. It extends to the post-match meeting with the umpire who has been observed. He tries to keep his comments focused and constructive. 'Make it as short as possible – ten or 15 minutes. You don't want a lecture for an hour about your umpiring after a long day in the field.' He is aware of the danger that the assessor's presence will deflect the umpire from behaving as he normally might. Finding himself assessing an umpire whom he had not originally expected to be watching, Tommy remembers introducing himself at the tea interval. 'He says, "Oh dear, don't tell me I'm being assessed." I said, "Yes, you're being observed." He didn't know who I was, which was a good thing. I said, "All I want is a chat with you after the game. Now don't change anything. Don't be looking for me. I move about."' Assessed umpires receive the detailed report on their performance. They have the chance to comment on what has been said. Occasionally the assessment form is passed on with a long essay attached, but more often umpires are content to accept the judgement of a peer and grateful to learn from the observations passed.

The method by which umpires for the Minor Counties Championship are chosen has changed over the years. When Tommy first joined the list, he had required support from his county and the decision to appoint him had come from MCC, soon to be replaced by the TCCB, where for many years Brian Langley dealt with all umpiring matters. In 1983 David Armstrong took over as secretary of the MCCA, soon becoming its first official to earn an honorarium. Armstrong came with a playing career behind him that included a couple of appearances in the Second Eleven Championship for Surrey, where he was assistant secretary to Geoffrey Howard. The second came when coach Arthur McIntyre, finding himself one short, prevailed upon him to leave his desk and play at Guildford alongside a young Bob Willis and Geoff Howarth against a Hampshire side that included a still unknown Gordon Greenidge. This exhilarating experience was not enough to persuade Armstrong to remain in London and he soon resumed a career in teaching that enabled him to devote long years to the service of Norfolk as well as the MCCA, where he was to remain secretary for 18 years.

The arrival of Armstrong determined the MCCA to run its own affairs and look after its own umpires. For some years captains had been marking the umpires at the end of each match, and these marks had been a crucial factor in determining who should stay on the list and who was to be axed. Under the Armstrong regime, the importance of the captains increased. All were at one time invited to a meeting at which their marks and reports across the previous season were made available and the ensuing discussion decided the fate of every umpire on the list. There could be stormy sessions. 'Captains were the power,' says Ken Shenton, 'I've known umpires give certain captains out and never return.'

There were two umpires' representatives at the meetings, latterly Tommy from the north and Paul Adams from the south. Paul carries clear memories of the procedures. 'Armstrong's regime was nothing if not transparent. We were invited in and sat round the table. All the reports were there. David Armstrong would have produced a list, a ranking order with percentage marks.' The meetings were held in November, and in the first week of

December a letter would go out to every umpire asking about his availability – if he had earned reappointment. 'And at the bottom, in fountain pen, was what your average mark from the captains was and where you came in the list. If you came in the top two, you knew that the following year you'd get a final.' Mention of getting 'a final' reflects the changes to the structure of minor county cricket from 1983 with the introduction of regional divisions and a play-off as well as the start of the limited-overs Trophy competition. Suddenly there were more rewards for the most highly regarded umpires, not just the match with the tourists, which would soon melt away.

Philip August, a former chief executive of Gloucestershire who had earlier worked for MCC at Lord's, joined the management committee of the MCCA in 2000, later taking on the post of competitions secretary, the second of two positions in the association that earns an honorarium. The son of a former chairman of the MCCA and distinguished Bedfordshire player, Philip himself played over ten years of championship cricket for the same county, later serving as its secretary. He now has responsibility for the administration of umpiring matters for the MCCA's championship and trophy matches.

There is no longer an annual meeting of captains to discuss the umpires. Philip explains that attendance had dwindled to the point where very few captains were bothering to come, but the advance of electronic communication has ensured that feedback is still gathered. A small committee now assembles under the chairmanship of former Suffolk captain Phil Caley, the MCCA's chairman of cricket. He communicates with all the captains, whose reports are sent in ahead of the meeting. Also round the table with Phil Caley and Philip August in deciding who the next season's officials shall be are Keith Coburn, an experienced minor county umpire and currently administrator of the Unicorns, as the minor counties representative side is now known, and Tommy, now titled umpires representative for the MCCA. Also invited to attend are Nick Cousins and Hughie Evans, both representing the ECB ACO.

Giving Tommy an official post in the MCCA came about in the aftermath of disbanding the Minor Counties Umpires Association, of which he had been chairman for many years. Formed in David Armstrong's days by a small group with Roddy Wilson as the first chairman, shortly to be replaced by Tommy, and including Brian Harrison and a good friend of Tommy, Dr David Fawkner-Corbett, who was soon installed as secretary, the association continued to arrange regular meeting for the umpires each year until 2012, when Phil Caley and Philip August felt that they should take it over so that it would become an official MCCA pre-season meeting.

It is widely recognised that the ACO has had aspirations to integrate all umpiring appointments below first-class and that minor counties cricket still represents the top of the pyramid for the recreational umpire. Moreover, for Chris Kelly at the ECB, there would be some logic if his remit on umpiring in first-class cricket and its one-day spin offs extended to taking care of the minor counties. Whilst the MCCA has no wish to cede responsibility for its umpires to either the ECB or ACO, the invitation to Cousins and Evans to join the committee enables advantage to be taken of the knowledge and opinions of the ACO performance and appointments sub-committee, at which potential D list umpires and those already on the list come under close scrutiny. Emphasising that Tommy has a finger in so many umpiring pies, he is one of the two performance officers on this small group along with Hughie Evans.

'Nobody's fallen out over it and we retain control,' Philip August says in emphasising the MCCA's wish to continue running its own umpiring. He also points out that the ECB or ACO might not welcome some of the problems if either were ever to take over the administration. He thinks, for instance, of the telephone call at seven on a Sunday morning that he answered in the hope that he had found an urgently needed replacement for an umpire who had been rushed to hospital the previous night. 'No such luck – it was another bugger dropping out with a stiff neck! And we've got a match starting at 11 o'clock! I can't see that anybody at ECB would be there on a Saturday night or Sunday morning. So it's better to keep it in house with volunteers.' As one with a finger on the pulse, knowing where umpires live and who may be in a position to take a couple of days off work, Tommy agrees – he knows what is involved in finding a replacement at short notice when working with part-time umpires. David Armstrong confirms that it was ever so. He once rang an umpire to tell him of an emergency appointment late in the day only to discover that the supposed colleague of the man to whom he was talking had committed suicide.

Addressing the question of which umpires should be on their list, the committee still take full account of the captains' marks and reports in their deliberations, though the marks are not used as mechanically as might once have been the case. Philip August points out that, while some captains are harsh markers, others seem to be kind to all umpires. He names a county. 'Had an umpire done only two matches and had they both been with that county, he'd be qualifying to stand in one of the finals. And we thought that's not quite right.' In Philip's eyes, some captains regard reporting 'as a tick box exercise' whereas there are others 'who think about it and write some really valuable observations.' Philip is also aware of a potential in-built bias where a losing captain will mark less favourably than a winning one. 'Sometimes you don't have to look at the score sheet to see who won the game – you look at the captain's report!' He also believes that, with appeals increasingly coming in from all parts of the field, new umpires are put under particular pressure, whereas the familiar faces are given an easier ride. Philip mentions a longer-standing umpire. 'Now he's a good man manager, reacts well to the players. They think, oh, he's all right – they don't even think about the game and whether he's made a mistake or two. They'll forgive him a mistake because he's a good bloke.'

There is now a more important role for boundary observations of umpires, and this is where Tommy comes in. Formal assessments play their part, though the notion that these should be carried out incognito makes Philip laugh if Tommy is to be involved. 'I tell him "Well of course they know you're here, Tommy. You've spoken to everyone in sight and we can all see you hobbling round the ground."' Philip sees a danger in formal assessments playing too great a part in rating an umpire. Inability to pass judgement on most decisions, he feels, can lead to peripheral aspects of umpiring playing too great a part. 'Assessing whether the signals are correct – the players couldn't give a monkey's about the signals. All they want is for the decisions to be correct.' He has also seen play suspended when it has been barely spitting, believing that the umpires were keener to impress those observing them than to apply common sense and get on with the game. And he remembers a county secretary close to incandescent at how many extra folk with clipboards had turned up. 'Three assessors, all with their wives, and all expecting lunch!' 'That was when we were training assessors,' Tommy pleads.

Less formal chat therefore plays its part, especially as several secretaries are ex-players and can give good feedback to the likes of Phil Caley, Keith Coburn and Tommy as they tour the grounds in their different roles. 'It's feedback from people whose views we value,' says Philip. 'We see who the best umpires are and give them the games. They may have had poor marks for a game, but for the wrong reasons.' Philip pays particular tribute to Tommy, who earns very little even when carrying out formal assessment duties, but who will be seen on minor county grounds for the sheer pleasure of watching a game. 'If he's not specifically requested by MCCA to go to a game, he still goes. He takes his lunch and watches the cricket and just likes to be involved.'

At the close of the season Tommy also plays a part in processing all the marks Philip August has collected, looking through captains' comments and scrutinising the assessment forms where an umpire has been watched. Where a weakness is detected or some counselling is needed, Tommy picks up the telephone. In Philip August's words, 'He talks to the umpire about the issues without naming the captain or the game, but it doesn't take Einstein to work which it probably is. He does it very well and in a way that none of the umpires take umbrage that he phoned up saying they'd had a bloody awful game or something. He does it in a nice way.'

At Bretherton it is not just Tommy but also Barbara playing a crucial role in making sense of all the marks that have been gathered in. It is not always the easy task it might seem. 'I've got one here,' Barbara says, 'he's ticked all the boxes as unsatisfactory then he's given him 100%!' 'Another report,' says Tommy, still ensuring confidentiality for the captain concerned, 'the umpire's had a good season in championship cricket, but in one knock-out game he got seven lbws wrong. I thought it was a misprint. He made seven poor decisions!'

Tommy is also involved with planning the schedule of appointments before the start of the season, a task he once undertook over a couple of days together with Keith Coburn. Now Philip August does the main part of the work, but the plan for the season is sent to Tommy, who likes to ensure that newcomers are standing with someone experienced and that no-one is exposed too often to the same county. He also tries to make sure that the practicalities of travel don't break the budget or impose needlessly tiring journeys on those who may have been engaged in a league match the day before the start of Sunday's championship game.

In recent decades the minor counties game has undergone many changes. Where once there were settled sides and players might enjoy careers lasting 15 years or more, now there are fewer familiar faces each year. Behind the change has been a move to three-day cricket, introduced in 2001. With matches nearly always starting on a Sunday, this change has meant that players have been required to take time off work for both Monday and Tuesday. In a less easy-going working environment this has often proved difficult for those in regular employment, while the trend towards younger players – those on vacation from university and the like – has been reinforced by ECB regulations offering the counties strong financial incentives to play at least nine men under the age of 26. There are still two places available for older hands, whose contribution Philip August believes to be very important. 'You need some senior players to talk about how you go about a run chase, how you look to try to bowl someone out in the fourth innings, which is alien to young cricketers brought up on a diet of limited-overs cricket.'

Just as the turnover of players has accelerated, so it has with the umpires. Ken Shenton has calculated that between 1994 and 2004 about 85% of the panel remained constant, but over the next ten years only three umpires have survived. Gone, it seems, are the days when others like Tommy – Brian Harrison, Roddy Wilson, Stan Levison and Bob Duckett – clocked up over 100 matches, their presence bringing its own reassurance before a match started. Some of the pleasure of the job has also diminished, Ken feels: 'With the two-day game you tended to have regular sides and you built up a relationship with the players. Now you don't know the players; and the youngsters, they haven't the gravitas of the older players – they've been schooled in league cricket rather than the gentlemen's game of minor county cricket.' Notwithstanding Ken's point Keith Coburn stresses that it was tough in a different way in the old days when so many of the counties had two or three players with experience of the first-class game, players who were hard but fair and had come to expect good umpiring, and there were tough and able club cricketers like Arthur Sutton at Cheshire who did not give umpires an easy ride.

Tommy and others like Ken Shenton and Paul Adams believe that promotion to the minor counties is sometimes too swift. 'People come with the idea that two- and three- day cricket is a doddle,' says Ken, 'but it's not.' Keith Coburn regards the three-day game as particularly testing for umpires, a very different challenge from their Saturdays in the league. 'Now on the third day you've got the pitch turning with fielders round the bat.' Tommy and other top umpires spoken to would agree that judging the bat-pad catches the fielders are hoping for is perhaps the hardest part of decision making. Ken Shenton adds that there is also more to sort out off the field, 'whether it be mowing the wicket or keeping ahead of the rain or whatever. It's a big step and too many are going on and too many are going down too quickly. You're losing umpires.' Tommy agrees: 'I can think of one young umpire who should have been forced to stop in his league for a couple of seasons to get more experience before going on to the minor counties and finding it tough and not enjoying it.'

The current situation, they all feel, is that there have been too many umpires on the list and that has meant too many have to be given too few games. 'The reason English first-class umpires are the best in the world,' says Keith Coburn, 'is that they are doing it all summer.' By the same token he feels it is asking a lot of an umpire to stand in only a couple of games in minor counties. Sometimes newcomers are dropped before they have had time to prove themselves. They are brought on, viewed with suspicion by the players and struggle. Keith Coburn has no doubts: 'The overall standard of umpires in the minor counties has dropped.' Tommy is less sure about the drop, but he and the appointments committee are seeking to improve the overall standard in 2015, when the panel will be smaller with the best of the umpires getting more games. Moreover, the trial of a 20-over competition with three counties coming together on a number of grounds around the country and three matches played in the day will provide extra opportunities for umpires, of whom there will be three at each venue.

Tommy beside the school trophy cabinet with his Lancashire Cricket Board OSCA, one of many awards to come his way

Chapter Fourteen

Service beyond the game of cricket

A brass plaque on one of the doors at Bretherton CE Primary School denotes the Wilson Suite. A library where the children can retire to read, it is testament to the part Tommy has played and the high esteem in which he is held at the school he once rode past on his home-made truck with its pram wheels. His first involvement had been for 12 years as a representative of the parish council, when he was described as a manager rather than a governor. There were only six managers, who met once each term under the chairmanship of the vicar, and in those days little was expected of them until a new head teacher had to be appointed. In 1995, when Tommy returned, this time as a governor, things were very different for the 14 men and women now involved.

On his retirement from running the shop, Tommy had been persuaded to return to the parish council on which he had previously served for over 20 years, and he resumed as their representative on the school's governing body. Before long the council-nominated governor was dispensed with, but by this time Tommy was friendly with various people working in the local Anglican diocese of Blackburn, and it is now as one of the diocesan representatives that he holds his position on the board.

The chairman of governors when Tommy re-joined was the incumbent of the local Anglican church, Bishop Donald Nestor. The bishop's title related to an earlier appointment in Southern Africa. He had been educated and ordained in England, but moved out to Africa in 1972, serving as chaplain at the universities of Botswana, Lesotho and Swaziland before being appointed to the suffragan bishopric of Lesotho in 1979. In 1992 he returned to England, becoming vicar of Bretherton whilst also acting as an assistant bishop in the Blackburn diocese. In 2001 Bishop Nestor moved to Durham to join the monastic Society of the Sacred Mission. With a new chairman needed, the bishop asked Tommy to take over. 'What about the vice-chairman?' Tommy had replied. 'She doesn't want to do it,' the bishop told him. 'Isn't there somebody better than me?' Tommy pleaded. 'Anyway I don't go to your church.' 'But you do go to church and you are a Christian – and that's what matters,' the bishop said firmly. There was no election – the job was simply passed on by the outgoing chairman. 'Now there's a rigmarole with a secret ballot,' Tommy comments, not bothering to add that the new democratic procedure still comes up with the same solution – he has continued in office ever since the bishop departed.

It is small wonder that this is so. Nick Ward has been head teacher for the past five years of a school that can boast an Ofsted rating of outstanding on 15 different counts and was ranked, in 2014, eighth best primary in Lancashire and number 73 out of 15,000 schools across the country. The head teacher has no doubt that he is exceptionally well served and supported by Tommy. 'You couldn't get a better chair of governors,' he says, going on to stress how well Tommy is known around the village and the range of activities with which he helps in the school, running PTA events and involving himself with the school's games club. Moreover, Tommy goes down to the school on Thursday afternoon and Friday each week to help in the office, a practice that began when the school bursar was taken ill and Tommy filled in while she was away. Nick Ward adds that whenever he needs support or advice, Tommy is on hand. 'He takes it ever so seriously and if there are ever any questions, I've only to ask him. It's just amazing what he does.'

Helping with the games side of the school has enabled Tommy to pass on his love of cricket by organising coaching and bringing in Kwik Cricket, a soft ball introduction to the game for young children with a playing format designed to bring maximum participation for all within a short games period. Bretherton has taken part in a cricket festival with seven other schools, and in 2004 the team brought back the cup to sit in a cabinet that had previously displayed only football and rugby trophies. It was to be the first year of a string of successes for boys' and girls' teams including a Kwik Cricket county final in 2007 that was played at Old Trafford.

The small school is able to admit only 15 children each year. In 2014 there were 59 applications for these places. Any visitor to the school will soon see why this is so. Cheerful and attentive boys and girls throng the classrooms where the rap over the knuckles of Tommy's childhood has long been a thing of the past. In an age where success is all too readily measured in material rewards for beating the next man, there is a tangible ethos of community life in the school, an appreciation of the value of helping others, neatly encapsulated in the school's mission statement: 'Learning together, growing together, achieving together, caring together, within our Christian family.'

Privileged to attend a special morning assembly when a much-loved vicar was bidding farewell before retirement, one could experience the ethos of the school in a way no prospectus could adequately convey. The children gathered and sat in rows in their well-appointed hall where the words that decorated the walls were: Hope, Truthful, Respect, Courage, Thankfulness, Friendship, Honesty and Companionship. A candle was lit, a simple hymn was sung and the vicar addressed the children. The parting message from Reverend David, as he was known, was that whatever you were going to be in life – whether accountant, nurse or footballer – there was also the wider and more important question: what kind of person will you be? Marking the departure of a man whose visits were clearly a high point of school life, each of the school's four classes presented him with a specially designed card.

Bretherton CE Primary may be a small local school, but its newsletter for 6th October 2014 carried an item that showed it has its place on the world stage. 'Wow! Congratulations to Joe Cairns, who last week was not only the Mathletics top student in the UK, but also number 1 in the world! That really is some achievement! Well done Joe!' And we older folk don't even know what mathletics might be, but it sounds like young Joe could become the kind of umpire who could carry Duckworth Lewis in his head.

The big change in Tommy and Barbara's life came when they decided that the time had come to sell the shop. Hayley looks back on her father's years as a village shopkeeper: 'He has always had a strong work ethic and was always busy. We had a fabulous upbringing being the daughters of the sweet shop owner, which made me very popular at primary school, and everyone wanted to walk home with me via my dad's shop.' By 1995 small independent shops were struggling to survive across the country, but Tommy and Barbara had always understood the needs of the local village and they had a viable business. 'We'd really struggled for years, but it was doing as well as it ever had at the end,' says Tommy.

Keen to retain the shop as a local amenity, the parish church decided to buy the building and the stock, though they were not permitted to pay anything for the goodwill. The plan was to install a paid manager with volunteer helpers. The shop traded on for three years, but the expertise of Tommy and Barbara was missing. 'Volunteers were fine for selling things,' Tommy explains, 'but they had no idea about buying.' He had offered to help in the early days, but found the new owners set on their own ideas. Where Tommy had used his liquor licence to sell cans of beer, cheap wine and the occasional bottle of whisky, suddenly the shop was stocking vintage wines at prices twice what Tommy had been charging. 'It didn't work,' he says sadly. Greengroceries had always been a strong line for Tommy in a village poorly served by a bus service to the nearest supermarkets, but the new management switched emphasis away from fresh produce to devote the space to racks of magazines.

Selling the shop gave Tommy and Barbara the chance to move home. Using the money from the sale and what they were able to get for the home in which they had lived since their marriage, they were able to bid for the two-bedroom bungalow which had previously been the home of an aunt, who was no longer able to live independently. The bungalow was rewired, given new windows and doors and Tommy and Barbara moved in in August 1996.

There has never been money for lavish living, but they decided that they should make one grand trip overseas. One winter they flew to Australia and New Zealand. In New Zealand there had been high hopes of seeing some international cricket, but the coach in which they were travelling got behind schedule and they arrived in Wellington at five in the evening just as an ODI was finishing.

In 2007 Tommy was persuaded to stand as an independent candidate on Chorley District Council for his local ward of Lostock, so named after the river that flows by the village. The council boundaries had been redefined in 2002, after which there was a four-year period when Chorley had no party in overall control until the Conservatives secured a majority of three in 2006. Lostock, comprising the three villages of Bretherton, Croston and Ulnes Walton, has an entitlement to two of the 47 seats on the council. Back in 2002, an independent, Margaret Iddon, had topped the poll with a Conservative, Doreen Dickinson, also elected, a second Tory and two Labour candidates being unsuccessful. With elections taking place in a third of the seats in 2003, Mrs Dickinson held off her only opponent, from Labour, and in 2004, when it was Margaret Iddon's turn to defend her seat, she defeated a Conservative and a Labour candidate.

In 2007 Mrs Dickinson's turn came round again and Tommy's hope was to unseat her and give Lostock a second independent alongside Margaret Iddon on a council where only three seats were not in the hands of one of the main political parties. He campaigned on strictly local issues that affected the three villages in the Lostock ward, his leaflet listing three priorities: traffic issues, particularly the number of HGVs travelling through the villages; improved local public transport facilities; more activities for young people.

Tommy has never been closely involved with any political party, but he counts Lindsay Hoyle, the Labour Member of Parliament for Chorley, a good friend. Until the boundaries were redefined, putting Bretherton into the Conservative-held Ribble Valley, he had been Tommy's MP; and, whenever Hoyle had needed premises for his surgeries, Tommy, knowing his preference for holding them in a community building, had arranged for the snooker hall to be available for him. When word of Tommy's intentions to stand reached Hoyle, steps were taken to withdraw the Labour candidate, the party wisely judging that Tommy had a much better chance of unseating the Tory. 'We're going to get you in,' Hoyle said. Tommy also recognised that in a largely Conservative village his own prospects would be damaged if he stood under Labour's colours, and he may have suffered when a rumour with a grain of truth circulated that he was being backed by Labour.

Tommy remembers the excitement of the count. Bretherton was clearly behind its former shopkeeper, but it was the smallest of the three villages that comprise the ward. Croston, about three times bigger, was the home territory of Mrs Dickinson and, to Tommy's surprise, he seemed to be more or less level with the sitting councillor in that village. But with Ulnes Walton it was a different matter. This was true blue territory. 'I think there's more horses than people in Ulnes Walton,' Tommy says. 'I bet I didn't get two votes.' The final figures were: Doreen Dickinson 745; Tommy Wilson 700. If just 23 people had voted the other way, he would have become Councillor Wilson. 'In a way now I am quite pleased' he says, reflecting on the time he would have needed to devote to council business. 'I wouldn't have been able to be dashing down to Lord's and I wouldn't have been able to give the time that I do now to my umpire observing.' The school would certainly have been losers as well.

Tommy has not played bowls for some 15 years because of back problems, and Barbara has also given the game up because of her back. But they both remain closely involved with the club, still acting as non-playing captains, while Tommy is in the middle of his two-year term as president. They are also to be found socialising or playing bingo or dominoes at the snooker club, where there has been a bar since the 1980s, and which has now become part of a fuller sporting 'complex' for the village. There is a football club and a recently created recreation ground, with Tommy predictably involved on the committee responsible for its inception. Sited on land at the back of Tommy's home, it is across the road from the cricket club and within easy reach of The Blue Anchor, to which the snooker players always repaired before they had their own bar.

For all Tommy's involvement in the wider activities in and around Bretherton, he and Barbara remain devoted to their family. Their two daughters and their families live at different ends of the village of Euxton, some six miles to the east of Bretherton. Fifteen years ago Hayley and her husband, Richard Stephens, started a weekly disco for young people in the village, giving them somewhere to go and enjoy themselves in a safe environment. Tommy and Barbara have been tireless in supporting the venture, going over each week to help, with Barbara running the tuck shop and making regular visits to the local wholesaler to keep it stocked. 'They have never missed a week,' says Hayley, 'often returning from holiday early to ensure they made it for the disco so as not to let the children down.'

Hayley is employed as a higher level teaching assistant. She often works with pupils with disabilities and special educational needs. 'I always stress to them that they can achieve anything they want to and do anything they want to,' she says. 'There are no barriers, and this I truly believe because of my dad's attitude and what he achieved and is still achieving in his life.' Richard, who is now partially sighted, works as a counsellor in a local high school and in private practice. They have a daughter Nicole, who is still at school. Hayley has two daughters by an earlier marriage, Jade and Justine, whose graduation photographs adorn Tommy's living room. Jade went on to work as a teacher in the leisure and tourism industry. She has a one-year-old daughter, Caydence. Justine now lives in south Oxfordshire. A social worker in children's services, she is shortly to marry Mike, a senior aircraftman in the RAF.

Tommy and Barbara's younger daughter Marie works in hospital administration at Chorley, while her husband, Neil Helm, is in social services working with people with learning difficulties. Their son, Tom, works for a bearings supplies company. He and his partner Holly have an infant daughter Ellie, a second great-grandchild for Tommy and Barbara.

The family at Christmas 2014
Back: Marie and Hayley; Seated: Nicole, Tommy, Barbara and Justine
In front: Tom with Ellie and Jade with Caydence

Chapter Fifteen

So what makes a good umpire like Tommy?

'What makes a good umpire?' When I have posed this simple question in the course of writing this book, the answer has invariably been conflated with the response to a parallel enquiry: 'What makes Tommy a good umpire?' Whatever qualities an umpire may bring, whatever his on-field personality, it seems universally accepted that underpinning the reputation of all well-regarded umpires is good decision making. And in the words of Paul Adams, 'To get those finals Tommy must have come high in the captains' marks – he must have been a good decision maker.' Philip August, with the benefit of having kept wicket in matches Tommy umpired, would strongly agree, while Alan Wilson with scores of matches for Netherfield in the league and for Cumberland says that Tommy was 'a very, very good umpire.' 'It's amazing how he got into position for run outs,' Alan adds, joining the list of those who have admired Tommy's ability to make so little of his infirmity. 'It wasn't an issue,' says Paul. 'One would have noticed if your colleague at the bowler's end was carrying a leg affected by polio and was struggling to get in position for run outs. I didn't, so he must have got where he needed to.'

These impressions of Tommy's mobility chime in with the views of his daughter Hayley in the wider context of life: 'My dad's disability was so insignificant in our lives that for years as a small child I didn't even realise he had one, which is crazy as it is so obvious; but I could never understand why children stared at him when we were outside the village. As I grew older this staring by other children used to make me really angry and I remember defiantly staring back at them. There was nothing my dad would not attempt to do, even the dads' race at sports day. In fact I cannot remember a single moment from my childhood when I had to say my dad couldn't do something because of his disability. Because his disability was so insignificant in our lives I didn't even think about it at all. Our lives were all so normal.'

For most people who have known Tommy well, the disability is patent but it has not seriously impaired his ability to carry out his umpiring and other duties. Thus David Armstrong links Tommy and Paul Adams at the top of the tree among MCCA umpires, but he cites Tommy's physical impediment in placing Paul as number one. Perhaps at the very highest level Tommy was not quite quick enough. No-one speaks higher of his ability, integrity and sincerity of intent than John Hampshire, who played major innings and captained Yorkshire while Tommy was officiating, and later stood with him in early rounds of the NatWest. 'If it hadn't been for his impediment, he would have gone on to be a very, very good first-class umpire,' John says. However, he felt that 'Tommy was always going to struggle to turn, and it could have been a nightmare when someone was taking a daft run.' Ray Julian shares the view that Tommy 'was a damn good umpire,' but also goes on to say of his infirmity that 'it did hamper him a bit.' Perhaps Ray's views were conditioned by the memory of sharing a room at Kendal. 'Do you mind if I take my leg off?' was Tommy's opening request that night and Ray then realised the extent of his disability. In fact, Tommy is aware that the sight of what he may jocularly refer to as his spare leg, when secured in its case, can give a false impression of the extent of his incapacity. 'He looked as if he was carrying a rifle,' Alan Wilson commented in talking of when he gave Tommy a lift to Leicester. Yet what Tommy wears is a calliper – it is not a false leg!

Tommy himself accepts that there is, perhaps always has been, some restriction in his movement. Certainly as he umpires on into his mid-seventies he has no illusions: 'They know I can't get square on, but I get in a position where I can see, and the majority of captains would say, "But he's a good decision maker." That counts for a lot.' Tommy's decision making took him onto the first-class list, but it didn't enable him to stay there. If his marks in his one full season were indifferent, it seems that he spent the summer without attracting much adverse criticism. Brief conversations with several players who took part in games in which he stood, including five captains in matches marked by memorable events or controversy, have served to emphasise how little notice may be taken of an umpire doing a quietly effective job. Always friendly and wishing to help, most of the players spoken to were almost embarrassed that they seemed to have taken the umpires for granted, that a man with a bit of a limp had not been better remembered.

It suggests that the limp was not so pronounced as to be a trademark, as it undoubtedly was for Roddy Wilson with his stick. Roger Knight, one of the captains spoken to, has clear recollections of Roddy officiating, but not Tommy. He remembers Robin Jackman saying that, with the new fitness tests for umpires that were just coming in around that time, there was no way Roddy could have passed and that he was not able to move well enough to get in position for run outs. John Hampshire goes further: 'It was a huge mistake. Roddy Wilson should never have been on the list.' But there is little evidence of the same strictures applying to Tommy, reinforcing his own feeling at the time that it had been his misfortune that two umpires with a disability should have been taken onto the first-class list at precisely the same time.

At all levels of the game a new umpire is doing well if he attracts no comment from those whose games he has officiated. With the passage of time his personality and little idiosyncrasies may begin to make a mark, for better or worse. Those umpires who have become legends of first-class cricket, as Tommy has in minor counties circles, did not do it in a single season. Chester, Buller, Bird, Shepherd, Gould....five very different characters, all respected umpires, but all with a reputation built up over many years standing in the middle.

Discussing decision making with a number of leading umpires emphasises the importance of what has been called 'selling your decisions' – persuading the players that a decision was the right one. It can be a matter of luck. Paul Adams remembers the luck falling his way in only his second minor counties match back in 1987. Chris Old, recently retired from the first-class game and playing for Northumberland, was opening the bowling against Suffolk on the first morning. A ball flashed through past bat and pad and flicked something. But what had it touched? 'I hadn't a clue,' Paul now admits. Uncertain, he ruled in the batsman's favour. There was clear disappointment from the fielding side with one of the short legs asking the batsman if he was not going to walk off. Old had said nothing until the wicket-keeper asked what he thought. 'It flicked his shirt – top decision!' said the former England bowler. 'In that instant,' says Paul, 'amongst the players – the batsman who knew he hadn't hit it and the fielders who had been told by a Test player that he hadn't hit it – my credibility was taking root. They knew I'd got it right and I'd had the courage to say "Not out." It was luck that it happened in the first session.' Told this story, Bob White, with over 300 first-class games as an umpire, suggests that a sixth sense may have helped Paul that day, much as Dickie Bird, from a hospitality box, is able to cite the fielders' body language as evidence when a catch is referred for judgement by television.

Alan Wilson remembers Tommy telling him: 'I watch their eyes. If they look straight at me, I reckon they're out!' Confidence is evident when an umpire neither rushes nor dithers. Taking time over a decision was the hallmark of Steve Bucknor when he was one of the world's leading umpires, and Bob White, who rated Paul Gibb the best umpire from his playing days, relates how Gibb always considered his decisions before giving his verdict. Perhaps revealing of how today's umpires are viewed, Bob suggests that his own decisions would have been better had he taken more time over them, time to play the action back in his mind. 'But the modern player thinks it's a sign of weakness – that you're unsure.' 'Probably very true that,' says Tommy. 'If you dither, they don't like it. If you fire them out, you're not taking enough time. If you take too long, then it must be not out. What we teach now is to go one, two, three, then give them out. That's the ideal.'

To the technical excellence of Tommy's umpiring must be added the personality that has stamped him out from the crowd. David Armstrong points out that 'he had such an equable temperament,' while Paul Adams says, 'If you add in that lovely avuncular persona, I can see how he would endear himself to the players.' John Hampshire speaks in similar vein of 'a typical Lancastrian, chatty and humorous, a terrific guy to know.' Perhaps Tommy belonged to an age where there was less tension between sportsmen and officials and more chance for post-match fraternising. 'In those days,' says Philip August of his own playing career, 'you'd have a beer with the umpires at the close of play and enjoy their company. Tommy was always one of those who was happy to talk about the game and talk about decisions.'

Mere geniality, though, is not enough. The best umpires above all are respected, as Tommy was in the eyes of Keith Coburn. 'And you earn respect,' he adds. 'You are not given it by rights.' It comes with gauging the mood of a match. Paul Adams, as a former school teacher, believes that those from his profession, like police officers, have a useful background for controlling a game of cricket 'if their man management skills have been properly honed and developed. Equally they can be disastrous if they can't ever forget about being a schoolmaster or a policeman.' Paul believes his teaching experience has helped in 'knowing when to turn a deaf ear and walk away with a player letting off steam.' Ken Shenton expresses similar sentiments: 'You have to know the laws and how to apply them in the right place and at the right time. You need law 43, common sense. You have to have a feel for the game. Tommy had that, but also a love of the game.'

The ability to remain calm under pressure, not being overawed or bullied by big name players, having the confidence to make a decision and stick with it are characteristics Ken would expect to find in a good umpire, and again Tommy meets the specification, whilst still being at times provocative in defending his corner. This last characteristic speaks of a man who has never been one to shirk confrontation in cricket or in the wider canopy of life, as daughter Hayley has grown up to appreciate: 'He believes that everyone has a right to voice their opinion about anything and he likes a good debate. My father and I are like peas in a pod and this has often caused clashes between us because we are so alike. Everyone was encouraged to speak their mind in our house regardless of age or subject so it was a very lively house.' Hayley's words ring true when she adds: 'But, for the amount of arguing that went on in our house, there was always an equal amount of abundant laughter.'

Tommy, Keith Coburn maintains, is a stickler for the laws, perhaps to a fault. He built his minor county reputation at a time when there were some strong and knowledgeable characters to be controlled, and the experience serves him in good stead with the miscreants of today's more boorish league cricket. 'I've got another one on Level 2 (offence),' Keith can remember Tommy being happy to announce. Hughie Evans makes a similar point, citing the awarding of penalty runs as an example of where Tommy leads the pack in applying laws to control the game. Fourteen years after penalty runs were introduced, Hughie has still to make his first award, but not so Tommy. 'He won't stand any nonsense with bowlers in the protected area and batters running down the pitch.'

No ball-tampering when Tommy is around
Tommy with Ken Shenton at Penrith, 1998

Tommy believes that standards of behaviour in league cricket have declined in recent years, and he is not one to let abuse go unpunished. He has reported players for abuse of equipment when bats have been thrown in the air to express feelings about adverse decisions, and he has even had recent cause to report a captain for assault. Nor was he happy to sit back when he felt that umpires in the Northern League were not being properly supported after reporting serious incidents. 'Players were being reported for bad behaviour, but they were only fined league points or given suspended sentences. There wasn't the discipline code we have today.'

After a particularly bad incident in an end of season match in the late 1990s, a meeting of the league's umpires was called before the first match the following year. All were sworn to secrecy as a proposal was put forward that, for the first round of matches in the league's first division, there would be no umpires. This draconian measure failed to win a majority in a secret ballot, but when the motion was toned down to imposing a boycott on just the worst offending club, the plan was approved. 'We said that we wouldn't turn up for their first or second team games. They'd have no umpires, and they'd want to know why. And we'd tell them why.'

Scheduled to take the first team's match, Tommy had a day off, while his good friend Ken Shenton also stayed at home instead of travelling to take charge of the second team game. As had been expected, telephones were soon buzzing. It was Ken who fielded a call from Radio Lancashire as the story of umpires going on strike made the national press. 'From that day onwards things changed,' says Tommy.

Not to have played the game at approaching the level of the match he is officiating is widely regarded as a severe disadvantage for any umpire. 'Yet with Tommy you wouldn't know that he had never played the game,' says Hughie Evans, himself a minor counties player with Cumberland, while Ken Shenton maintains that 'in some ways he reads the game far better than most people who have played it.' This feel for the game makes Tommy a strong man manager, and enables him to uphold the laws and impose the standards he believes are right. As Hughie points out, such disciplinarians often don't get far because the players don't like them, but Tommy manages still to be well respected and liked.

While the old hands in the umpiring community are saddened to see newer entrants too often motivated by vanity or prestige, it is Tommy's love of the game that communicates itself to all who come into contact with him. 'He likes everything around cricket. He has a passion for the game,' says Philip August. 'And all the work he does for minor counties cricket, he doesn't get a penny piece for it.' This often selfless devotion to the cause has brought a string of awards. In June 2009 Tommy was chosen by Lancashire Cricket Board from three short-listed candidates to receive an OSCA (Outstanding Service to Cricket Award) in the 'Outside the Scorebox' category. The presentation dinner at Old Trafford was followed later in the year by another at the Paradise Room in Blackpool, where Tommy's services to cricket won him a Lifetime Achievement Award from Lancashire Sport. Between these two awards he was in the Nursery Pavilion at Lord's for the ECB's own OSCAs ceremony, one of four ACO members nominated. Following the presentations to mark his 25 and 34 years in the middle as a minor counties umpire, in 2012 he was made one of only seven Honorary Life Members of the MCCA, matching his life membership of ACO.

Yet, for all his pride in the recognition he has been accorded, it typifies Tommy's deep-rooted love of the game that, entering the last years of his eighth decade, he is still bent on extending his unbroken years of officiating in the Northern League, his heart set on a record that may prove unmatchable. Meanwhile it remains his involvement with young umpires that brings him particular pleasure. It was youngsters who first chanted, 'There's only one Tommy Wilson.' It is young umpires who can still empathise with that sentiment. 'So you're writing a book about Tommy Wilson,' one teenager said when a trio of ACO Young Officials attended a gathering of older umpires. Assuring me that they would be buying it, they made plain what Tommy's mentoring and good humour, as well as all his stories, had meant to them.

Let his daughter Hayley have the final word: 'I think the biggest influence my dad has had on me is his attitude to life – that there is nothing you cannot do if you put your mind to it regardless of any disability you may have.'

INDEX